Corporate Divestment

Corporate Divestment

Gordon Bing

Gulf Publishing Company
Book Division
Houston, London, Paris, Tokyo

Corporate Divestment

Library of Congress
Catalog Card Number
77-86528
ISBN 0-87201-141-0

Contents

Preface

Sales of subsidiaries, divisions, and product lines are complex transactions constituting a significant portion of merger and acquisition activity quite different from sales of independent privately or publicly held businesses. The sellers remain in business rather than retire wealthy and do not become employees but continue as employers. Usually, the divestiture involves less than a complete, autonomous business and may be interrelated with the remaining business of the seller. The seller must aggressively seek out and persuade the prospects to buy instead of being courted to agreement. Frequently, the subsidiary has serious operational problems that create an element of urgency, limits the number of prospects who would be interested in buying, and causes the seller to make difficult and unpleasant decisions.

Divestiture is the antithesis of an expansion move and is a way out of a problem. Management may want to rid itself once and for all of a recurring problem or troublesome marginal operation. Divestiture is usually a one-shot affair to clean up a specific condition. However, it may be a one-time massive program to give the business a totally new direction by eliminating major product lines or business activity in a geographical region. A new management may feel compelled to demonstrate itself to be action oriented and wipe the slate clean of prior management errors through a combination of divestitures, write-offs, and the establishment of reserves that will nearly assure future profits. Strategic long-term planning may play a role, but for most companies divestitures are a singular event associated with failure. Few companies have a well-defined, continuous program for systematic evaluation of operations that will routinely lead to early profitable divestment decisions, let alone an established procedure for implementation. Managements seldom have the experience to conduct a sale in the most advantageous manner because few have had the opportunity to gain experience both in divestitures and the complex general management skills required by modern business enterprises. In fact, a management with substantial divestment experience often carries the unwanted reputation of low operating competence.

Divestitures can result in great benefits for the seller, the buyer, and the employees. For the seller it is an opportunity to redeploy the assets of the corporation into areas considered to be more productive. It frees management's time and, in some cases, provides the corporation with the financial respite to recover and resume growth. The process can also prove to be a total failure.

For a buyer the divestment is an opportunity to enter a field thought to be worthwhile, a chance to broaden overall capability and demonstrate to the public tangible rapid growth, a challenge to the management, and often a chance to prove the seller wrong. It may also prove the buyer's judgment to be poor.

For the employees it is a whole new future. The seller in most cases is disenchanted with the subsidiary and an unsatisfactory relationship exists. The very human tendency of rationalizing one's shortcomings by blaming others has done its work. A new owner provides the opportunity for a new spirit and relationship. It may also produce a period of tension and conflict, because the buyer will undoubtedly assume he knows more about what he acquired than he actually does.

This book is primarily a handbook for owners, directors, and managers who are considering the divestiture of a subsidiary, division, or product line. It does not dwell on the wisdom of the decision to divest but rather on how to make the most of the decision. While many are carefully considered, there is ample evidence that not all are made on a logical basis as a result of comprehensive studies of the subsidiary, its problems, and alternate solutions. Furthermore, the decision to divest is often made with little thought of how it is to be accomplished and the executives faced for the first time with the task of implementation may be as bewildered as if asked to build a moon rocket. In other cases a decision to divest is not made because of ignorance about how to carry out a program of divestiture.

For those embarking on a program of sale or those who have received an unsolicited proposal to sell a subsidiary, this book is a checklist and detailed description of a program on what must be taken into account and how to proceed. Knowledge of how to divest should give sellers confidence that they can successfully divest and reduce their reluctance to do so.

An executive checklist in summary form is provided in the Appendix for managers who are pressed for time and as a means of final review. The emphasis is on all that must be done and how to do it. The facts of a specific situation and competent executive business judgment are ingredients the reader must add to make the numerous decisions to produce a successful program.

The book is primarily written for the American seller who desires to divest of a subsidiary in the United States or abroad. References to tax or legal considerations and accounting policies are based on current practices in the United States. Such policies are subject to change and may be, but probably all are not, applicable if the divestiture is international or the seller is not American. In any divestiture it is of critical importance for the seller to have up-to-date tax, legal, and accounting advice for whatever countries are involved and this can only come from practicing professionals of the highest ability. Regardless, the overall approach described and factors to be considered are generally applicable for sellers domiciled in any country.

A potential buyer will also find the book to be helpful in a careful evaluation of a divestiture. While the book is organized from the seller's point of view, it also becomes indirectly a list of matters the buyer must consider.

A note on the terminology is in order. The terms "subsidiary," "division," and "product line" are used somewhat interchangeably throughout the book. Whichever is used at a particular time is thought to be most appropriate, but the reader should keep in mind that either of the other two terms probably could be used equally well. In most cases the term "subsidiary" is used. While subsidiaries of corporations are legal entities, so many interlocking and dependent relationships with the parent usually exist that most could more accurately be described as divisions or even product lines. "Divestiture" is used in the narrow sense of transferring ownership by means of a sale of a going business, unless otherwise defined. The use of masculine pronouns throughout the text is certainly not to deny the substantial contribution of women in the business world.

Gordon Bing
January, 1978

1.
Divestment Alternatives

Divestiture of a subsidiary, division, or product line may be attractive for many reasons or combination of conditions, each of which requires a thorough, unemotional evaluation to determine if it is a solution superior to other alternatives. The owner may need greater liquidity, less financial obligations, or may be making basic changes in business strategy and no longer wishes to remain in the business. The sale may be government induced as occurs in antitrust litigation or through expropriation proceedings. New government regulations on environmental conditions, worker security, worker participation, or trade regulations may make the business too difficult to continue. Labor relations difficulties, increased wage costs, and declining levels of productivity can discourage an owner. Restrictions on repatriation of profits may be too severe. The competition may be too strong. Parent company guarantees to the subsidiary may be too great or involve unacceptable risks. The product or service may have become or is soon to become obsolete with capital requirements too large to restore the business. A loss of confidence in the long-term future of the business may prevail. The owner may not have the management competence, depth, or time to properly direct and assist the subsidiary. The subsidiary may have lost money, is now losing money, or is expected to soon become unprofitable. A poor financial condition or outlook is undoubtedly the most common reason, and the condition a cautious prospective buyer will suspect until convinced otherwise. Regardless of the reasons for considering divestiture, the potential seller should guard against hasty decisions and consider what is to be accomplished, what will be the full impact of a sale, what is to be sold, what alternatives would be a superior means to achieve the seller's objectives, and what is the probability of success for each alternative.

1

Define Objectives

An owner's objective to improve his cash position or eliminate debt can be reached to varying degrees through divestments. Sales of assets, such as subsidiaries, is one answer for some companies seeking to solve their capital shortage problems. The more profitable a subsidiary, the greater are the odds it can be sold quickly for cash, while unprofitable subsidiaries are difficult to sell for cash and seldom can be sold rapidly except at a distress price. However, the immediacy of a corporate cash problem is often incompatible with a long sales program. A firm threatened with or in bankruptcy can hardly spend time studying the wisdom of a divestiture or hold out for a top price.

A seller looking to solve cash difficulties through divestiture should remember that the primary purpose is to raise cash and not just rationalize the disposal of a problem subsidiary. However, if cash can be raised and other problems solved, all the better. The divestiture of a subsidiary, to be worthwhile, should produce more cash than can be raised either by liquidation or by continued operation of the subsidiary. A subsidiary sold for cash will produce cash for the seller only once, and the loss of potential future operational profits must be taken into account. Regardless of the uncertainties and elimination of future operational profits, the divestiture of subsidiaries has on many occasions produced the cash to solve a seller's financial problems and permitted the seller time to recover and become stronger than ever. Even the existence of an active program of divestiture may be adequate to give comfort to creditors and cause them to delay more aggressive action.

Many executives periodically review the businesses they manage for financial performance and fulfillment of short and long range policy objectives. The evaluation of existing businesses and studies regarding their future and desirability of retention are usually far more extensive than those that initiated the business in the first place. If more thought had been given originally, there would be fewer divestiture candidates today. Often a business that never should have been started or acquired was the result of one person's enthusiasm, and today is unprofitable or does not relate to the main business or both. Since management tends to be preoccupied with immediate problems, it becomes convenient to leave the future to others and seek the assistance of elaborate planning departments, staffed with highly educated professionals who endeavor to perceive trends, peer into the future, and provide advice based upon their observations. These planners have varying levels of competence or luck, depending on one's point of view, ranging from skills in backward planning or second guessing to a real ability to look ahead and forecast with uncanny accuracy. The staff planners also have the problem that despite their belief in their superior wisdom, chief executive officers are more inclined to listen to and take the advice of operating managers, particularly those successfully managing profitable subsidiaries. Regardless, their conclusions may eventually lead to divestment decisions.

Frequently, decisions regarding long-range markets and goals are the result of pressing current problems rather than extraordinary insight into the future. It is an easy but not necessarily wise management decision that involves little controversy or foresight to exclude a profitless or marginal subsidiary from long-range plans. It is a very difficult, controversial decision to sell off a presently profitable business because management believes the long-range outlook to be bleak. This is true even when the subsidiary's business clearly no longer relates to the rest of the corporation. Every management would like to have the perfect warning system that alerts it to operations that will deteriorate in the future and prior to potential buyers discerning the same fact, but such a foolproof system is yet to be devised. The dubious reliability of market research studies often contributes to the controversy rather than resolving it, but such studies do lend an aura of objective analysis to the decision and provide less accessible third parties to blame in case the decision to sell or not to sell ultimately proves to be bad. Even loss of confidence in the subsidiary because of technological obsolescence may only mean obsolescence in the markets presently served and is not necessarily a reason for divestiture. A subsidiary profitable today has time to improve and develop its technology in order to compete in tomorrow's market and such technological progress is for most companies a fundamental and routine aspect of being in business.

Rightly or wrongly, continual growth is a standard criterion by which corporations are judged and executives judge themselves. A board of directors may readily agree with its management's recommendation or conclude independently a corporation temporarily lacks the management depth or competence to enter into new proposed ventures regardless of their merits. Less frequently, they conclude the total corporation is too diverse to manage and control and take steps to reduce its scope.

Such decisions undoubtedly should be taken more often. Management talent is a scarce commodity, and a corporation is wise to use its management to maximum advantage without overextension and to do so priorities must be set. Talented executives cannot readily be found and employed. Years are required to develop an effective management team and while this process is in progress, it is prudent to make best use of what is available. The cause of almost every divestiture situation can be traced to a management error and there is no need to compound the errors by making more. A lack of adequate management time to manage a subsidiary is a common reason for divestiture and the lack of time usually becomes apparent when management finds itself spending a disproportionate amount of time on the subsidiary.

Management may be in short supply and so also may be the financial resources necessary to support the business. A subsidiary losing money may require infusions of cash just to keep it afloat and to protect the existing investment until either profits return or it can be disposed of. Businesses with products dependent upon their development of advanced technology or products subject to frequent improvements or modifications require large amounts of capital to be competitive. The eventual return on this investment may have a degree of uncertainty which the owner cannot afford, or the owner believes his capital could produce a greater return in other areas. If a substantial investment has been made in a new product but more capital is required to bring the product to market or maintain its competitiveness and more funds cannot be committed by the present owner, then divestiture may provide the best chance for recovery of the investment. Intense competition is not the fault of the subsidiary's owner, who should view the competition as a condition to be evaluated, which may or may not be possible to overcome, rather than as a challenge which must be met regardless of cost. In some situations competition is too strong and it is hopeless to attempt to compete regardless of the amounts of capital poured in. Divestitures because of capital requirements usually occur when the parent company's management has a low opinion of the subsidiary's long term prospects. Most managements probably could raise the capital if the opportunity and returns were great enough.

Compulsory divestitures as a result of government action or court decisions are relatively common but complicated situations. Here the seller's objective is to comply with authorities by divesting, but at a convenient time and for an attractive price. Usually the only certain factor is that the divestiture must occur within a fixed time period subject to possible extension. How the sale will be accomplished, the price, the terms of sale, and who the buyer will be are details for the unfortunate owner to work out. Many of these details may also be subject to further court or government approval. In a divestiture of this type there is usually ample publicity to attract prospects, and the seller is never in a position of attempting to explain to a skeptic why the subsidiary is for sale.

Another type of government induced divestiture is an expropriation. Expropriation often does not occur in the familiar all at once method that makes the headlines, but creeps in through the devices of compulsory profit sharing, worker participation, requirements for local directors, and restrictions on financing. The seller's objective in expropriation is to secure the maximum price and avoid any further investment. The involuntary seller has few bargaining advantages and time is not one of them. A divestiture as a result of threatened or actual expropriation is an exercise in political intrigue few business executives are equipped to handle. Most faced with this problem should seek outside help from attorneys who have actually had experience. They also should contact other companies for advice which have been through similar proceedings.

No statistics exist, but there is no doubt the most common objective of divestitures is the improvement of the seller's economic position through elimination of current or anticipated marginal profits or lack of profits. The subsidiary's poor performance may be caused by any number of factors ranging from bad management to bad markets but the end result is a bad bottom line on the financial statement that the seller will no longer tolerate. Sales because of losses are so prevalent that, when subsidiaries are experiencing poor financial results, talk of divestiture in the parent and in the subsidiary tend to develop automatically. Even when responsible executives in the parent company are not giving the slightest thought to divesting the subsidiary, it is such a logical concomitant of unsatisfactory financial performance that sale rumors spring up. Prospective buyers will assume poor financial condition or major concealed defects to be the true state of affairs until convinced otherwise. A poor financial history of a subsidiary need not be a deterrent for either a seller or a buyer, because it is future earnings in the final analysis that counts most. However, past performance is considered one guide to the future so it cannot be ignored. The seller must convince a buyer of "new factors" to discount the past, because the factors and conditions that caused the unsatisfactory performance and decision to sell will seldom be convincing reasons for someone to buy. The actual decision to sell may be triggered by factors unrelated to the subsidiary's poor performance, such as losses in the seller's other operations that eliminated the earnings shelter and made intolerable the luxury of carrying a losing operation.

Evaluation of Alternatives

Regardless of the reasons to be contemplating the divestment of a subsidiary, before making a final decision to do so the alternatives should be explored. Unfortunately, unless a willing buyer is available, the results of a divestiture sale program are no more or less predictable with certainty than most other alternatives. The evaluation of alternatives also identifies feasible courses of action and sets contingent plans in the event a sale program fails.

Each alternative should be compared with divestiture by sale on a basis of probable success and downside risk. How the comparative studies will be accomplished will vary with the resources, experience, and sophistication of the seller, and will be influenced by the size and importance of the subsidiary. The depth of the studies and caliber of the participants will be in proportion to the importance of the subsidiary. Extensive studies do not ensure wise decisions; but an understanding of the condition of the subsidiary and its business environment coupled with an evaluation of the alternatives should improve the probability that the decision eventually made will be the right one to achieve the owner's objectives. While management whims and prejudices rather than cold logic may very well decide a subsidiary's fate, and often do, it is reasonable to assume comprehensive studies will produce no worse, and it is hoped better, decisions than those arrived at by other means.

Ideally, a study team would conduct the evaluation of alternatives. The team should have as its charter, the responsibility for an objective evaluation of existing conditions and all possible alternatives and be free from internal political pressures to develop support for a specific alternative or suppress information on past or current conditions. The team's work will be more valuable and less controversial if its emphasis is on current conditions and the future instead of concentrating on who is responsible for the problems. If an unbiased and independent study is impossible, then the seller may as well proceed as planned all along and save the time and expense of the study. It is not uncommon for the decision to sell to be made and then a study requested to prove the decision correct with those participating in the study knowing full well any other result will be at their peril. An independent study team must possess or have ready access to individuals knowledgeable in accounting, financial analysis, law, and the operation of businesses similar to the subsidiary. They will have to call upon the full range of disciplines associated with business to perform the comprehensive study required.

The team's first task will be to determine the condition of the subsidiary and this will probably prove to be a more formidable task than anticipated. In some instances it may prove nearly impossible as with remote and neglected foreign subsidiaries and in most cases, some surprises will emerge. An understanding of the market and political/social environment in which the subsidiary functions must also be determined and reasonable forecasts for these external factors developed, all of which may be difficult. Regardless, a determined effort should be made to ascertain the current conditions as a base from which to evaluate alternatives. Using the present condition of the subsidiary as a base, a model or forecast showing the results of each alternative can be prepared. These results should make the decision as to which course to follow relatively easy or, at a minimum, narrow the choices. It is recommended that a study team be given a rigid time schedule for completion of their activity and final decisions reserved for a time after their work is complete.

The general categories of alternatives to divestiture by direct sale that should be reviewed to determine if they are practical and superior solutions are as follows:

1. Retain the subsidiary and not sell and:
   - improve operations
   - run on static basis
   - run and phase down or out
2. Liquidation
3. Shutdown and "mothball" facilities
4. Take the subsidiary "public "
5. Divest by issuing subsidiary stock to shareholders of parent
6. Bring in new shareholders
7. Abandonment of the subsidiary
8. Any combination of the above
9. Any combination of the above and divestiture by sale

Retaining the Business

Retention of the business is an alternative to continuously evaluate before, during, and after a decision to sell is made. Businesses are not easily created, and a management would do well to think twice before it gives one up. Talk of selling the losers and using the cash to buy winners is largely management bravado far easier said than done. Matters may easily have reached the point where everyone in management is talking only liquidation or divestment because it appears to be an obvious solution and often is thought to be the politically acceptable line. If there is divestiture talk, then management is probably "down" on the subsidiary and aspiring ambitious managers will find it easier to go along with the divestiture advocates rather than argue against, because retention may more readily prove them wrong.

Regardless of management attitudes, it may be financially advantageous to retain a marginally profitable or even modestly unprofitable subsidiary with a positive cash flow than it is to shut it down or spin it off. Retention of a marginal or unprofitable business which would command a price less than book value also eliminates the need to report a loss on the divestiture, which the seller may be unwilling to take. Retaining a subsidiary can take various forms with any of three general operating policies. It may be run with full support and an all-out effort to improve its performance. This approach usually calls for an infusion of capital or management or both since programs based only on "doing better" do not have a reputation for a high probability of success, particularly when a subsidiary has been in financial difficulty. This total support approach could involve changing the entire nature of the business with new products or services.

A second approach would be to retain the subsidiary and run it on a static base without drastic changes or infusion of money and talent. Frequently, this approach is coupled with an attitude of wait and see, which can prevail when management is unable or unwilling to make a divestment decision at the time. This static approach may be the only one practical when strong government policies preclude sale or liquidation.

The third approach is to retain but start a program to reduce the scale of the business to a more satisfactory level or to prepare to eventually phase it out at a later date. Running down the business may also reduce its size so that it is more readily saleable or liquidated. This approach has particular application for a manufacturing subsidiary with a large inventory of material, parts, or work in process that can best be sold as finished goods or in countries where severe obligations to employees exist.

Liquidation

An outright liquidation may appear to be the quickest approach, but it is only advisable if losses are unbearable or there is no possible way to operate the business at a profit or at all, as would be the case if severe and uneconomical environmental regulations were enforced. Even in a bankruptcy, the creditors will be better off if the viable portions of the business are sold as a going business rather than liquidated. However, a liquidation program should be seriously considered if a comprehensive study and forecast shows the business will not be profitable for two or more years. The owner should face up to the fact that if there is no way to run the business at a profit, it cannot be sold at a price for other than liquidation value and only liquidation is feasible. An exception is the case where the subsidiary is located in a country where the government is more concerned with employment levels than with the economic health of a particular business. A government may take action to prevent a liquidation and also become a prime prospect to purchase the subsidiary, but there is a growing reluctance of governments to take over sick companies.

Liquidation is not as quick or easy a process as it may seem. It takes time to find buyers for the assets and during that time many costs continue. There are obligations to employees, inventory liquidation problems, requirements to complete work in progress and fill existing customer orders, continuing warranty obligations, and the necessity of handling all the various other legal obligations associated with the business. The problems and obligations are not transferred to a buyer as is the case in a divestment. A complicating factor is that the seller's representatives handling the liquidation will quickly find themselves dealing with professional liquidators famous for their bargaining skills but not all known for integrity. This can prove to be an unequal contest in which the seller will find it very difficult to realize the true value of his assets.

In certain cases, an "asset heavy" subsidiary may be shut down and liquidated more profitably than it is to divest it. This occurs largely because of time considerations and continuing unacceptable losses or the existence of extremely valuable assets, producing little income, which may or may not be required by the business. It may even be possible to sell the valuable assets separately and retain the basic business or sell the business in a separate transaction. Valuable assets, if included in a sale of the business, would be reflected in pricing since tangible assets reduce the buyer's risk and the buyer could have the cash benefits from any liquidation that occurs. However, most buyer's emphasis in determining what they will pay will normally be concentrated on expected return on investment, and they will have little interest in the liquidation of assets unless that is their business.

Mothballing

Shutdown and placing a subsidiary in mothballs or on a standby basis is practical if the parent is financially strong and a reasonable possibility exists for demand and adequate price levels to return. Application of this approach is fairly well limited to defense, mining, basic metal, and food or chemical processing plants. Shutdown and mothballing should not be considered without also evaluating the problems of starting the business again and the standby costs to make start-up possible. During the shutdown period, certain amounts of maintenance are required and security must be established to protect the assets, and the associated costs of these necessary services may be prohibitive. Eventual start-up will involve reassembling a management team and workforce, which can be difficult under the best of circumstances. Unless the company can pull its management teams from other operating units it owns, start-up will be very costly. For most businesses, it is not a feasible solution.

Share Transfers

"Going public" as a means of divestiture with a public offering of shares for cash has, in the United States, very little application and less chance of success. It usually is advocated by executives who have not the slightest idea of what is involved. For the market to accept the shares, the subsidiary would have to have a very strong earnings record and continued strong expectations or possess some new technology of great promise and if either condition existed, there would be little reason for the seller to divest. The market's doubtful enthusiasm for new issues of this type, the expense, the legal, accounting, and SEC requirements plus the time involved make "going public" a most unlikely alternative. A short discussion with a knowledgeable and reputable attorney or CPA usually will be adequate to discourage interest in this approach. The approach may have some chance outside the United States where the government would assist because of nationalistic policies and a program of promoting local ownership.

Divestiture by issuing the stock of the subsidiary to the shareholders of the present owners is possible if the business is a totally autonomous corporation. From a practical standpoint, the subsidiary must be profitable and if it is, the recipient shareholders will probably have few objections. If the stock of the parent is publicly traded, then the shareholders will expect a marketable security and the usual high costs of an SEC registration will be incurred. Distributions of this type are considered dividends by the parent company but they may be structured on a tax free basis for both the parent and the recipients of stock. This alternative is limited to situations where special conditions exist. It has the advantage of eliminating the problem of finding and negotiating with prospects. It also has characteristics of only transferring assets from the left pant pocket to the right pant pocket.

The possibility of going public with a subsidiary as a means of divestiture is highly unlikely, but another comparable alternative, which may have merit, is that of selling less than 100% of the subsidiary. Creative and imaginative thinking on this possibility may produce the best possible alternative. A willingness on the part of the seller to retain some equity is also a way of emphasizing to prospects that the seller believes the subsidiary has a bright future. A newly created joint venture of this type can be particularly attractive if the new partner in the venture is strong and adds to the venture ingredients previously missing. This may be in the form of management techniques, new technology, local nationals with good contacts, capital, or marketing outlets. Foreign prospects could be particularly interested in this approach because of the continuity provided by the seller. The seller has advantages in that it is a means of securing some cash for the subsidiary and yet retain a portion of the business. From a financial accounting standpoint, this approach can be advantageous in that the subsidiary becomes an unconsolidated subsidiary with its debt removed from the balance sheet. The joint venture may be far more viable than the old wholly owned subsidiary and a 50% interest becomes more valuable than the prior 100%.

Abandonment

Outright abandonment of the subsidiary is worth considering under certain circumstances and it may even be the only practical alternative. If the subsidiary is soon to become unprofitable or presently is unprofitable and there is little prospect of a return to profitability and the assets are not readily saleable for an amount in excess of the liabilities, then abandonment is a possibility providing there are no parent company guarantees, technology, or material supply dependence that would preclude such a move. In the absence of parent company guarantees or obligations, the owner would know the value of his investment and the amount of his loss, which could be written off against current income, but he must conduct a complete search to make certain no guarantees exist. The owner would have to assess public reaction to an abandonment, which could be anywhere from insignificant to extreme animosity or delight. Abandonment usually takes the form of a cessation of financial support, which would throw the subsidiary into some form of receivership, government ownership, or be taken over by creditors. If the owner walked away from a small subsidiary in a remote foreign country, the action would probably have little impact on the owner's other businesses. However, if the subsidiary abandoned was in the same country as the owner's other businesses, the adverse impact would be of such severity that abandonment would be impossible. The creditors would be very alarmed.

If abandonment is possible, then the owner must carefully plan his timing and actions prior to either the date of announcing the cessation of support or the date it becomes apparent the owner will no longer provide support. The owner may be better off to just stop support rather than make a formal announcement. Prior to the time of support cessation, the owner should determine the practicality of removing any valuable assets including cash from the subsidiary. The owner also must consider the safety of key employees and make certain they are not endangered by the action and if so, make arrangements for their safety. Physical removal from the country may be the only safe approach. The abandonment alternative is most common for subsidiaries located in countries other than where the owner is located. The threat of abandonment may force solution of problems that could never be solved without a crisis. The threat may also cause changes in government policies, such as taxes or import duties, or induce the host government to grant or guarantee loans that would enable the subsidiary to become a financial success. Many governments can be stirred to action by the prospect of more unemployment and a reduction in their country's economic base. A more gentle form of abandonment is to "give it away" or even pay someone to take it. This approach totally and legally separates the present owner from the subsidiary and is particularly applicable when the subsidiary's problems are a result of insurmountable government regulations.

Combination Alternatives

An objective evaluation of a subsidiary may demonstrate that a combination of several alternatives will be the owner's best solution. The larger and more diverse the subsidiary, the greater will be the probability that multiple solutions exist. A subsidiary with more than one physical location could conceivably evolve an approach where one location was retained, another liquidated, a third sold as a going business, and the overseas operations abandoned. Another variation especially applicable for foreign divestitures involves selling the assets and business, but retaining advantageous management contracts or licensing agreements. This easily could be more attractive financially than full ownership. The combination of alternatives will vary with each situation and a discerning management will not limit itself to the study of single solutions.

Selling as a Going Business

Divestment by sale of the subsidiary as a going business is the approach that normally will produce a greater benefit for the seller. If conditions will permit such a program, then by all means it should be attempted. If the present owner is unwilling or unable to successfully manage a subsidiary, that does not mean someone else would also fail. A new owner may bring exactly what is needed, as in the case of a sale to local nationals who better understand the market and have superior government contacts. If the results of the sales efforts are not promising after the program has been in progress a reasonable period, other alternatives can still be pursued.

Appendix A contains minimum data a seller should have for a preliminary determination of the feasibility of divesting a subsidiary and as a basis for studies to compare alternatives. This is only the minimum data for a preliminary decision on whether or not more extensive detailed studies are warranted, the results of which would likely demonstrate divestiture to be a sensible move. In most cases, the seller will have far more data available than are found in Appendix A and should utilize all available information. Much of the data in Appendix B will be helpful in the evaluation and decision process and eventually will be needed in the sales program. However, the seller should be on guard against the common affliction of paralysis through analysis. Demanding more information is a convenient way to avoid decisions and seldom will all information be available. The responsible executive will sort out what is absolutely necessary, accept any information that is readily available, and then make a decision.

A realistic evaluation of the price and the type of cash, notes or stock which may be received as a result of a divestiture is critical to compare alternatives. A subsidiary may have such limited expectations of future financial success or liabilities of such magnitude that it is either unsaleable at a price essential to the buyer or it may not be saleable at any price. The subsidiary must represent an investment for a buyer upon which a good return is anticipated. Consequently, the seller must be able to convince a buyer of the reasonableness of the price by describing conditions and an overall business plan under which a fair return will be received. The buyer's return on investment must be firmly kept in mind in establishing price expectations to avoid unwarranted grandiose hopes that have a nonexistent or extremely low probability. A seller should not be deluded and expect to find a buyer who is a wealthy fool. Information in Chapter 5 will assist a seller in estimating a realistic price to expect, thus facilitating the comparison of alternatives at early stages.

To evaluate alternatives, the seller must estimate the probability of finding a willing buyer by evaluating the more logical prospects for their degree of interest and financial ability. It may be advisable to meet with the most probable on a preliminary basis to learn if they would be serious prospects in the event a decision is made to sell. High probability prospects with businesses complimentary to that of the subsidiary will welcome the opportunity for tentative discussions and while they may eventually decline to buy, they will provide insight for the seller as to the chances of selling. Contacts of this type may also be handled satisfactorily by consultants or third parties so as not to directly involve the principals, but such caution is seldom warranted. Meetings with prospects to "test the water" will not only help establish the chances for a sale, but will provide the seller with information on who should be contacted first if the sale is planned.

A divestiture by sale will take considerable time to accomplish. Cash requirements or current losses, if the subsidiary is losing, may be of such magnitude that a long program will be untenable. Furthermore, a losing operation will be more difficult to sell. At an absolute minimum, it will take five months from start to closing and this would be exceptional time. The five-month minimum begins from the time the decision to sell is actually made, and it assumes substantial study and investigative work has already been accomplished. One can assume it will take at least a month to gather sufficient data before making the first presentations to prospective buyers. Another six to eight weeks minimum will be spent in presenting data to the prospects, showing the subsidiary and allowing the prospects time to evaluate the subsidiary and determine their position. Negotiations to reach agreement on terms may consume weeks, and it will take the attorneys five to six weeks to draw up and agree upon the necessary contract and related items for the parties to sign at closing. The seller would do well to assume it will take at least six months to effect a sale and have a closing; and, if it is accomplished in that time, he should be pleased. If the sale is to a foreign buyer, then the time period will be further extended.

A sales effort will bring the subsidiary under intense scrutiny such as never before. If the seller does not know the details of the subsidiary's business, potential buyers will surely learn them and either educate the seller or remain silent to the seller's detriment. A seller should question his knowledge of what really goes on in the subsidiary. Are the financial reports accurate and reliable? Does the subsidiary contain hidden assets and liabilities, such as undervalued assets, key patents, valuable leases or undisclosed bad debts, litigation, warranty problems, a nonexistent backlog, and the like? Do surprises continually surface? What is the overall quality of the management? Is there frequent turnover? Are forecasts and profit plans seldom met with the reasons unclear? If the parent company does not know the true conditions, it must learn what is going on in order to evaluate alternatives and before attempting a sales program. The study team will have a dual responsibility of developing complete accurate data on the subsidiary and to recommend any feasible alternatives.

Unsolicited Offers

Corporations are approached from time to time by potential buyers to learn if they would consider selling off a particular subsidiary.

These unsolicited contacts may occur for any number of reasons and at a time when the owner has given little or no thought to such a possibility. Such contacts may precipitate serious review of the subsidiary and the implications of a divestiture which could result from a decision to sell. The parent company would be wise not to make a decision to sell solely on the basis of an unsolicited request to sell. The sell decision should be made with the understanding that nothing may develop with the present prospect and once negotiations begin, the matter will not remain secret. A divestiture of this type still requires the large amount of investigative and other preparatory work necessary to conclude a sale. The seller, upon deciding to sell, should seriously consider a full program of selling to others in the event a sale is not consummated with the prospect who started it all.

The unsolicited contact requesting a corporation to sell a subsidiary should be treated initially with considerable caution. If the subsidiary is not for sale, then an unequivocal "not for sale" should be given. If there is interest in exploring the possibility, then the representative of the prospect should be told that sale might be given some consideration after a senior executive of the prospect came to visit the owner, presented credentials, and explained why the prospect wanted to buy the subsidiary. Only after such a meeting should a decision be made. This approach does not commit the seller in any way, and a determined prospect will gladly seize the opportunity to present this story and thus prove intent. If after such a meeting the decision is made to negotiate and sell, then all the preparatory work must be accomplished prior to setting a price and negotiations.

Few companies will have a well defined procedure for identifying potential divestment candidates and few will have the established internal systems and capability to implement a divestiture. Companies are planning for growth and success rather than contraction and how to get out of problems through total elimination of the problem operations. Until forced to seriously consider divestment, there is a natural reluctance to do so. Divestments are difficult and challenging but they need not be considered impossible or beyond the capability of most managements.

A decision to dispose of a subsidiary is one of the more important that a senior executive will ever be called upon to make or even recommend. It should not be done lightly without full review of the alternatives, an estimate of the probability of success, and an awareness of the impact of such a program. Jobs and careers of the subsidiary's employees are involved and whether the decision proves to be right or wrong, so will the career of the executive making the decision be affected. Those making the decision should utilize all the available talent to compare alternatives and evaluate the probable results.

High level internal task forces for this purpose may be created or outside consultants employed or a combination of both used to produce the optimum evaluation of the situation. The larger the transaction in relation to size of the seller, the more the time and expense for a comprehensive study can be justified, but in all divestitures, large and small, considerable care should be exercised. Regardless of the extent of the studies that led up to the decision, there will always remain an area of uncertainty, but once the decision is made to divest a subsidiary, much can be done to increase the probability of a short and successful divestiture program.

2.
Major
Problems

A final decision to enter into a divestiture sale program should not be made until the major problems associated with a sale have been thoroughly explored. These are problems of such magnitude that they could prevent a sale, make a sale totally uneconomical or create severe problems in the seller's other operations. These are problems that cannot be ignored since they will eventually surface during the selling process, negotiations, or immediately after a sale is consummated. While the list of major problems is lengthy, not all will be applicable to any given situation. The problems in most cases can be resolved with a proper effort, but in some situations they will preclude any possibility of a sale. It is best the potential seller learn very early if the situation has insurmountable problems rather than proceed with a hopeless program.

Debt and Equity Obligations

Most business organizations have debt in one form or another. This may be in the form of bank lines of credit, notes, debentures, bond issues, preferred securities, leases or any other type of debt or equity instrument lawyers and accountants can conceive. Along with the debt comes terms and loan provisions often of a complex and voluminous nature. These provisions are negotiated by lawyers, accountants, treasurers, and their like, but seldom directly by the chief executive or the board of directors who consequently may be unfamiliar with the terms in complete detail.

Creditors and investors strive for as much tangible security as they can possibly receive, and it is often given by company negotiators believing it to be relatively meaningless at the time granted or perhaps having little choice because of the need for the cash or credit. In some corporations, common or preferred shareholder consent may be required if the assets to be sold are significant. Therefore, a complete review of equity, security, and debt instruments is necessary to determine what approvals, if any, are required and from whom before a sale can be completed. Management's conviction that a divestiture is in the best interest of the corporation will not necessarily convince creditors it is in their best interest. Whenever approvals are required, they should be secured in writing. Should a sale involve a relatively small or insignificant part of the creditor's collateral, approval should not be too difficult to secure; but it can be very time consuming because of the lender's internal procedures. However, if the sale represents the potential disposal of a significant part of the creditor's security, then it is unlikely final approval will be given until one is very close to making the sale and then only after long negotiations. The creditors will want a voice in significant divestments as to price and how the proceeds from the sale will be utilized and may demand a heavy toll for giving approval.

Terms of sale will also be of interest to creditors. Whether the collateral is large or small in relation to total indebtedness, the seller should never assume approval will readily be given regardless of the seller's conviction about the reasonableness of the request. The price for approval required by creditors may take the form of demanding an overall renegotiation of the debt instruments or insistence that all proceeds from the sale be used to pay off or reduce the debt. Either condition may make the price too high and eliminate the divestment alternative. If the collateral secures notes or the debt instruments held by numerous creditors, then the approval problem will become particularly time consuming, difficult, and possibly unfeasible. The more creditors, the greater will be the difficulty in securing approval. A corporation must assess the probability of receiving timely approvals and develop appropriate procedures and approaches for securing the approvals. When the collateral to be sold and indebtedness is large, the chief executive may be required to personally negotiate with creditors because the chief executive normally will have the best chance of success. Regardless of who makes the approach, it should be made early, the program fully explained, and the approvals secured in writing.

Government Obligations

Other obligations may have been incurred from participation in government programs designed to assist businesses and encourage their growth. Tax concessions, investment grants, export subsidies, training grants, grants of land and other benefits of this type may have been accepted or utilized by the subsidiary. As a result of acceptance of these benefits, the subsidiary may have obligations and long-term commitments that would make divestiture impossible or financially unattractive. If any of these benefits were secured through special negotiations and not as benefits of general legislation, the reaction of the government to sale may be very strong indeed. A seller of a foreign subsidiary should check very carefully to see what he has gotten into since he may have made commitments in more optimistic times to remain in business indefinitely and these commitments can be fulfilled no other way. Aside from legal commitments, a seller will also have to evaluate any moral commitments that may exist. The conflict between social responsibility and economic responsibility may have no guidelines for resolution.

Parent Guarantees

Difficult problems may exist with the parent company's guarantees of obligations of the subsidiary being considered for divestment. The seller's desire to escape such guarantees may be the reason for selling the subsidiary. The guarantees may be for indebtedness of any type but most frequently for lines of credit. The guarantees also may be for performance bonds, leases, job performance, and various product and process warranties. The recipients of guarantees will not be eager to see them transferred to a financially weaker company and may not be agreeable under any circumstances to see them transferred. If one purpose of the sale is to eliminate the parent company's guarantees of the obligations of the subsidiary, then the sales program will have to concentrate on prospective buyers who are very strong financially. It also will be largely up to the recipients of the guarantees as to whether or not they are willing to see the guarantees transferred to another guarantor. Whatever parent company guarantees exist will have to be fully evaluated as to their transferability.

Potential buyers will be extremely reluctant to assume guarantees of the type where the extent of exposure is unknown as is the case with product or process warranty claims or litigation. They also prefer in general to buy the subsidiary as "clean" as possible, making retentions of guarantees by the seller an attractive approach. However, it is imprudent for a seller to retain guarantees over obligations and risks the seller no longer controls. In some cases it may not be possible to transfer the guarantees, and they may have to be retained to accomplish the sale or with the seller agreeing to indemnify the buyer for all or part of any ultimate losses.

Labor Relations

If a subsidiary is established as a full corporation and a union has a contract only with the subsidiary and there are no parent company guarantees, then bargaining is not necessary if the subsidiary is sold in its entirety as a corporate entity. In these cases the buyer automatically assumes the obligations of the union contract along with all other liabilities and assets of the subsidiary. However, if the contract is about to expire, the seller must disclose in the negotiations plans to sell or be subject to a bad faith bargaining charge. Many believe it is a good industrial relations practice to discuss the matter with the union even when the employer is not required to do so.

If the asset to be sold is a division or a product line and any of its employees are represented by a union, the seller is legally required to bargain with the union over both the decision to sell and also the effects upon the employees of a sale. This bargaining must occur even though the union contract is in full effect, and the sale is expected to be completed before its expiration. When bargaining is necessary, the law requires serious good faith bargaining to be conducted but it does not require an agreement be actually reached over either the decision or the effect. The failure to bargain can result in litigation and possibly prevention or reversal of the sale. The difference between good and bad faith in bargaining is not easy to define in any situation and is the issue in many NLRB cases and the subject of endless litigation. It is particularly awkward in divestment bargaining because the employer is under no obligation to agree to any demands of the union when the union is covered by a contract with a no-strike clause that precludes their use of a strike to enforce their demands.

Another complicating factor is that both sides are bargaining over a decision or discussing effects that may or may not happen. There is no certainty a buyer can be found nor does anyone know the plans of un-identified buyers. The unions may also believe any new owner will be better than the present and put up little resistance. These bargaining sessions in mid-contract take on a strange character, and about all the management representatives can do is state they are contemplating a sale and listen to anything the union has to say. What the union has to say will probably include its general estimate of management's overall competence. Then at a later meeting, the seller can announce the decision to either drop the idea or proceed to a selling program. The bargaining over the effects will be of the same nature but more complex because of the employees' concern for continuity of their rights and benefits although these transfer automatically because a buyer will take over the labor contract.

A seller will be wise to consult an attorney specializing in labor law throughout the bargaining or have him directly handle the bargaining process because of the complex nature of labor law. Communication and bargaining is not only legally required but is important for harmonious labor relations, an ingredient a buyer will insist upon. Sophisticated buyers are not willing to walk into a disagreeable labor atmosphere. If the bargaining occurs near the expiration of a union contract or a sales program is in effect when a contract expires, then an aggressive union may recognize its bargaining advantage and extract a significant price. A seller would do well to avoid attempting to sell a subsidiary near the expiration of its key union contracts. Each country has its own labor laws that must be considered in an international divestiture. The labor unions are primarily interested in the welfare of their members with top priority given to continuity of employment. If a sale of the subsidiary will result in no loss of jobs, there should be minimal difficulty in meeting obligations with the union. If divestment causes job cutbacks, extensive problems can be anticipated.

Former Shareholder Obligations

Many companies have been acquired under contingency or earnout type provisions with the purchase price variable and dependent upon future earnings of the subsidiary after the closing. Should the subsidiary to be divested have been acquired under such terms and the earnout period is not complete, then a difficult problem exists. Any earnout provision is an invitation to litigation, and, if the parent company decides to effect a sale of the subsidiary, the chances of litigation are greatly increased. Specific terms in original acquisition agreements providing for sale during the earnout period are almost nonexistent. Any attempt to negotiate in such terms would have caused doubts about the intent of the buyer and made him appear to be some sort of liquidator. At the time an acquisition is being concluded, the parties are seldom thinking of failure and a future divestment. The alternatives are to settle with the former shareholders on the best terms possible or attempt to continue on the earnout arrangement after completion of the sale. Cash contingency payments are transferable, but, if earnout arrangements involve issuance of stock, it is impractical to transfer the obligation to the buyer. Furthermore, a new owner is unlikely to be willing to disclose earnings without which it is impossible to calculate an earnout. However, this may be acceptable for some and become a condition of sale.

Another complicating factor is the lack in uniformity in business philosophy and methods of calculating income that could cause the buyers income data to be useless for earnout calculation purposes. In most cases the seller must contact the former shareholders prior to closing the sale and bring about a settlement of all claims for their earnout. The former shareholders may perceive this to be their opportunity to drive a hard bargain or even seek revenge. With the subsidiary again for sale as prima facie evidence it was a bad acquisition, chances are they are convinced the subsidiary has been mismanaged; they made a mistake in selling; and they dislike all or most of the seller's executives. The contact with the former shareholders should be by the executive with whom they have the best rapport if only a few shareholders are involved and personal contact is possible. A large group of shareholders will require mailings and methods of broader contact. The seller's bargaining position will be stronger if the approach is made in a context of the seller's wanting a settlement in the event he sells, rather than the seller's having a buyer and being able to sell only if he secures their agreement.

A related condition may exist if extremely firm and binding employment agreements are given to employees and particularly former owner-managers that not only state salary but also provide for specific executive positions to be held in the subsidiary. Employment agreements may be with the subsidiary alone, with the subsidiary but guaranteed by the parent, or in some cases, with the parent alone. A buyer may be unwilling to assume these agreements, and the employee may be unwilling to see the contract transferred. Again, it is a situation for compromises or litigation and one that must be settled.

Time to Sell

Realistically, the sales program and closing will require a minimum of five months after the first contacts are made and easily may take a year or more. Is everyone aware of the time required, and does the seller have the financial capacity to stay with a program of such uncertain duration? A seller must consider there always is a chance of failure and decide whether even a remote chance is an acceptable risk or if the program is one in which the potential benefits and costs involved are justified.

Relation to Total Corporation

The relationship of the subsidiary to the total corporation must be reviewed in depth. Does it have a supplier or a customer relationship to other subsidiaries that must be maintained? As an independent supplier or customer, the subsidiary sold may become very independent indeed and such independence could be an intolerable risk for the seller. Will a lack of control of such relationships or total loss of the relationship have serious adverse effects upon other operations? Will sale of one subsidiary eventually force the sale of other interrelated ones?

Once a sale is consummated, the basic relationships change to a degree not always fully appreciated by the parties during the cordial euphoria of the selling and negotiation process. As an example, pricing will no longer be under the seller's control; and new prices may create very difficult conditions. New prices can reflect more accurately the true economic values of the goods or services and may indicate prior accounting and financial analyses which justify the divestment to be erroneous. It is nearly impossible to write a long-term agreement covering a supplier-customer relationship that cannot be negated if either party becomes dissatisfied. Furthermore, laws have been enacted that restrict this type of agreement and limit exclusivity. It is safe to assume that unless the relationship continues to be advantageous to both parties, it will disintegrate regardless of any written agreements. The marketing relationships must be evaluated to determine if there is any duplication or overlap. Should the distribution system for the corporation involve multiline sales personnel, serving both retained subsidiaries and the subsidiary sold, then the loss of such sales or probability of continuing the multiline sales relationship must be carefully studied and solutions developed. Seldom will it be possible to continue the arrangement. Distribution through manufacturer's representatives or other independents can be adversely affected if multiline sales are involved, because it will no longer be possible to make as strong a demand for their time and efforts. It should also be ascertained whether or not there is a creditor or debtor relationship between the subsidiary for sale and other subsidiaries of the corporation. This type relationship will undoubtedly influence the sales price and terms of sale. A line of credit for an entire corporation may have provisions stating certain ratios and tangible assets must be maintained. This required borrowing base for the entire corporation could be jeopardized in a divestment involving substantial assets. The divestment may improve the overall financial condition of the company, but the lenders must be satisfied.

Creating a Competitor

Will the subsidiary once divested become a competitor? This possibility exists if the business to be sold is in the same business as other parts of the seller's organization. The problem could be very real where the subsidiary was in another country and sold to the government or local nationals who were fully supported by the government. All governments want to encourage exports and the development of

local industry. Unlimited government support could change a presently insignificant and unprofitable subsidiary into a formidable competitor in a relatively short time. The subsidiary may possess the
technology, specialized machinery, and know-how that would constitute an adequate base from which to build. A determined new
owner in collaboration with the government could find ways to void or
circumvent any licensing or territorial marketing agreements entered
into at time of sale if it is in the owner's advantage. Only continued
dependence upon the seller, usually for technology, will keep agreements intact and the seller must determine what other than legal
recourse exists to enforce dependence and compliance with the contracts.

Asset Limitations

Does a clear marketable title exist for all of the major assets? Real
estate included in the overall package for sale may present a particular problem if a clear title to the property does not exist. Title
searches should be started promptly for key real estate in order to
avoid last minute difficulties. Real estate owned by a subsidiary for
many years may present surprises in the title search no one
suspected. If problems with the title are found, it may become a time
consuming process to eliminate the title difficulties and delay or
negate a sale.

Real estate, motor vehicles, trucks, water and aircraft, machine
tools, office equipment, telephone equipment, computers, and even
employees are frequently leased. Whenever leases exist, they will
have to be reviewed to determine their tranferability. Many companies have enjoyed the financial leverage possible through leasing,
but leases can complicate sales and are not conducive to a quick sales
program. Whatever is leased must be disclosed early to prospects to
avoid an appearance of misrepresentation. Long-term real estate
leases may present particularly difficult problems or may be viewed
as an advantage depending upon the buyer's plans. Very short leases
or leases soon to expire on assets critical to the business may have to
be renegotiated prior to a sale. In some situations the buyer may look
favorably at a short lease as a chance to escape an unwanted liability.

Sale Impact on Corporation and Executives

When the subsidiary to be divested is a significant part of the total
corporation, the impact of the sale will change the corporation's
nature and many questions should be addressed prior to sale.

1. What will remain of the corporation?
2. In what direction is the corporation going after the sale?
3. Will a divestment reduce the momentum and synergy of the corporation?
4. Will it reduce the spread of risks over the entire corporation?
5. Will it remove from the product line a key segment making it impossible to provide a "complete package?"
6. Will divestment create hostile reactions and attitudes that will adversely affect other operations of the company?

These are questions that need comprehensive answers prior to a sale. The rush to dispose of a problem subsidiary or the prospect of a cash surplus may become so strong inadequate attention is given to what happens next. Just as divestments require months to complete, so do acquisitions, and a sold business will not be quickly or easily replaced by one more compatible or profitable. If the sale is a significant portion of the business, overhead reductions will be in order. Divisional or regional organizations may have to be terminated or combined. A combination of divestiture of loss or marginal subsidiaries and supporting overhead may be just the proper strategy to restore a corporation to financial health but it also may make future growth very difficult. The extent of reductions will be influenced by whatever plans the corporation has for use of the cash received from the sale of the subsidiary. When the subsidiary to be sold represents a major portion of the corporation's total assets, care to avoid violation of bulk sales laws must be exercised. These laws are designed to prevent exactly this type transaction if it will jeopardize the interests of creditors.

While each executive must personally assess this matter, the internal political effects of the sale cannot be ignored. Major shareholders, directors, or other key executives may voice strong objections to such a program or utilize the proposal to sell as an opportunity to settle other scores. Recommendations to effect a sale are often tantamount to either an admission of failure or an identification of someone who erred to the board of directors or fellow executives. Failures usually bring about questions like "Who got us into this mess?" and "Who has been responsible for that company?" It is hoped these questions can be answered with the universal scapegoat "prior management," but this may not be possible. Conditions can exist where executives may not be able to survive even a recommendation of divestiture. Often, discussion of divesting a subsidiary cannot occur until the executive responsible for acquiring, starting, or managing it is no longer affiliated with the company. Should the sale be controversial within the company, then the internal political problems will be all the more severe. These controversies should not continue beyond the time of decision and implementation when it no longer is an issue as to who is right and wrong. It must be certain as to who can make the decision to proceed or not to proceed, and this then will be the course followed. A strong chief executive, fully supported by the board of directors, will greatly facilitate a successful sales program.

Public Relations

The possible effect a sale would have on a corporation's public image will probably cause more anguish and be given more attention than deserved. This is particularly true in public companies where securities laws require disclosure of significant decisions and events. The rationale for the sale can be properly presented to the public, and the corporation's overall image can actually improve. Whatever are management's reasons for selling, it is most unlikely they are capricious or foolish, based on facts and conditions known to management at the time of the decision. Hindsight may prove it otherwise; but, at the moment, it is reasonable. A decision to sell at least indicates to the public the corporate management can be decisive and most of the public will attribute more wisdom to the corporate management than it deserves as well as assume the corporation has access to information others do not have.

However, in some cases the public image problem can be severe. This is true particularly when the subsidiary is a significant, profitable part of the total business. In such cases a sale may give the impression the company is actually going out of business or has major, not fully disclosed, financial problems. Government, public, and employee reaction can be strong when the business is important to the economy of a region or country and prospective buyers are not of the stature of the present owners. The seller also must be careful in public pronouncements on the reasons for selling in order to avoid scaring off the prospective buyers or causing embarrassment for the eventual buyer. A buyer does not wish to be placed in a public position and made to appear a fool by purchasing someone else's problems. Negative public reaction, which may ultimately involve the wrath of politicians, can easily occur if potential buyers are thought to be foreign. This reaction can discourage the foreign prospect, even if he is not prevented by direct action from buying.

Licensing and Marketing Agreements

Does the subsidiary have significant licensing and marketing agreements that are nontransferable or transferrable only with the approval of the other party? Agreements of this type are often of critical importance to a business, and the tangible assets are only of liquidation value. The business may be of little value or worthless if the agreements cannot be transferred. Licensing agreements may contain assignment provisions covering this contingency and permit ready transfer but most do not. The grantor of a license wants to know with whom business is being done to ensure maximum exploitation of a product or service. If the license is of value, it will not be easily transferred to a new owner. Therefore, a very early evaluation of this matter needs to be undertaken. If the license is nontransferrable, then an effort must be made to work out an agreement with the grantor. A grantor will probably not approve a transfer until it is known to whom the license is being transferred and the grantor has evaluated the new prospect and assessed the alternatives. There always is a question of when to notify a licensor or licensee. Premature notification may bring on troubles before a new owner is available. The seller will have to decide upon the timing after reviewing the written and unwritten agreements and assessing the general state of the relationship with the other party.

Tax Effects

The tax effects of the sale may be so severe that the advantage of sale will be negligible. This may particularly be the case if it is a subsidiary acquired in a tax-free stock exchange which has a very low base for tax purposes. A sale for cash can produce a cash tax liability of considerable proportions. A tax expert will be able to determine the impact of taxes on a sale under a variety of conditions, and such advice must be secured early. Tax considerations will effect the entire transaction including how the sale will be structured, the timing of the sale, and where the profits or losses should be taken.

Uncertain Liabilities

The existence of concealed liabilities or potential liabilities of a nature where their magnitude is unknown may delay or preclude a sale. Lawsuits or warranty claims against the subsidiary may be so great that the owner cannot relinquish control of his legal defenses, and a prudent buyer would never accept financial responsibility. This condition may easily exist when new products have been introduced but technical problems have emerged or market acceptance has been very slow with sales substantially below forecasted levels. Large jobs may be in progress with cost overruns highly probable but of unknown size. Negotiations with the customers for reimbursement under escalation clauses, value of change orders, or changes in the scope of jobs may be underway but have an uncertain outcome. New government regulations may be about to be announced which may or may not adversely affect the business. Such regulations also could have a favorable effect and provide an indirect recommendation of the product.

The subsidiary should be carefully reviewed to make certain there are no liabilities of unknown magnitude that would make sale at the present time impractical. Prospective buyers have little incentive to assume major risks when they do not have to do so. It is much easier for them to walk away.

Government Review

Justice Department, regulatory agency, or other governmental agency review and approval may be necessary for a sale. When approvals of this type are required, it would be highly unusual if the seller was not well aware of the condition. If the subsidiary has a substantial share of the market or it is a sale to a competitor that would reduce competition, then the seller can assume there will be government interest in the transaction. The sale of a marginal or loss business may only be possible to a competitor where it is hoped two halves will make a whole and as a result, competition could actually be increased, but government review may still be involved.

Past litigation may have produced settlements or consent decrees that require judicial review of the decision to sell and the transaction itself. In the transportation field, the appropriate regulatory agency will review the result of a sale and can exercise a veto power. The agency may also be a primary motivating factor in the sale if it believes such a sale would make a healthier industry. When the transaction is international in nature, government approvals may be necessary in one form or another. This can take on extreme forms as is the case in Canada where if a foreign business is sold that has a subsidiary in Canada, then approval under the Canadian Foreign Investment Review Act is required for the portion of the sale involving the Canadian subsidiary and this approval is far from automatically granted. Many other countries have similar or other procedures designed to control foreign investment.

Whenever review and approvals of either a governmental or judicial nature are required, the seller should evaluate their probable result very early. This can be done with a combination of review of policy statements, the state of the law and administrative rulings and usually with informal discussions which commit no one but provide guidelines as to what is possible. Appropriate discussions with political figures may also become desirable and when such is necessary, the seller's executives of highest rank will be most effective. The only certainty of outcome when governmental or judicial approvals are required is that the attorneys who eventually represent the participants will prosper.

Government policies on currency control and repatriation of profits may be so severe that the seller will be unable to receive the proceeds from a sale in a usable form. The proceeds could be in a soft currency that could only be spent within the country received and there its value would decline rapidly because of inflation. Since regulations of these matters vary greatly from country to country, whenever the contemplated divestiture is international, this should be an area for early seller review.

The seller must be sure that he/she truly has the will to go through a sales program. Is the seller willing to make the decisions, commit the time and resources, resolve the myriad of problems and issues, and provide the forceful direction to see the program through? It is easy to decide to sell, but to have knowledge of what is involved and the resolve and determination to go ahead until a successful conclusion is another matter entirely. These are questions which a potential seller should not lightly answer. The most important single factor in a successful sales program is the determination to see it through and face up to all the problems and develop and effect early solutions.

3.
Major
Questions

Potential problem areas of a magnitude that easily could preclude a sale have been discussed, but many other important questions must be resolved that are not of such dimensions but could readily negate a sales program. They are of sufficient importance that proper handling and early decisions will greatly facilitate the sales program and provide a business-as-usual atmosphere during the sales period plus aid in an orderly transition of ownership. These are problem areas which will eventually surface, and the decisions required can best be intelligently made in advance rather than at a time of crisis preceded by a period of rumors and fumbling ambivalence. All the participants, the buyer, the seller, and the employees involved must know the terms, conditions, and company policies that prevail. Failure to make advance decisions and provide a policy framework can only exacerbate a situation which by its very nature is full of unknowns.

Operating Policy

An overall policy and operational approach to managing a subsidiary during the sales period should be decided upon and presented in detail to all personnel. Prospective buyers will also insist upon knowing the nature of these policies. To present a more attractive saleable subsidiary, it is better to build it up and improve it during the sales period; but for a seller who wishes to dispose of the subsidiary without getting in any deeper, this is not always practical. The two points of view are not necessarily inconsistent or irreconcilable, but in the great majority of sales, compromises will have to be reached. It will be very difficult to sell a company on a financial downhill course where it continues to lose money or has increasing losses and nothing is being done to reverse the trend. It is discouraging to a buyer to see a facility in a state of disrepair, the absence of a marketing program, the reduction or elimination of engineering effort, reduced maintenance, no capital expenditures, inventories reduced to un-realistic levels and an absence of other activities essential to the future of the subsidiary. Of course, it is unwise for a seller to be com-mitting major funds to a subsidiary in the process of being sold or to be launching a subsidiary into new ventures that conceivably may be of no value or interest to a prospective buyer. In general, the best operational policy is along the lines of one where the seller continues to run the business and improve the business as though it would not be sold but refrains from making new major financial commitments, key personnel changes, or drastic changes in business approach and policy. The seller in setting his policies and making his decisions should not forget that the sales program is of uncertain duration and may not succeed at all.

Employee Involvement

The timing of notifying management and employees of the decision to sell the subsidiary must be planned. They should be informed early, so they can be brought into the program to assist. Furthermore, ex-perience has shown it to be nearly impossible and seldom necessary to keep a sales program a secret. Just the gathering of data to make the decision to sell will create enough rumors to convince many employees such a decision has already been made. Parent company executives often delude themselves into believing their subsidiary employees do not know or suspect what is going on but secrets are dif-ficult to maintain for any length of time in a business organization.

The notification decision and management involvement question is complicated in large organizations by the existence of levels of regional or divisional management between the president and the subsidiary. Regional or division management and subsidiary employees may prove to be an excellent source of sales prospects, provide key overlooked data on the subsidiary, make favorable presentations to prospects, and assist in many other ways during the sales program. Deceitful cover-up stories will preclude this valuable assistance. They may also provide the seller with information heretofore unknown by the board of directors or top management, which would call into question the entire rationale for selling.

Prospective buyers who become serious will sooner or later want to meet with the employees and secure their views. The purpose of such interviews will be readily apparent to most employees regardless of the ruse used. Personnel of some of the best prospects are probably already known to some employees, and their appearance to inspect operations and facilities will quickly give matters away. The greatest concern surrounding early employee notification is that they may quit if told the subsidiary is for sale. This should not happen if the seller honestly explains to his employees the reasons for contemplating the sale and points out the advantages of staying on. The major advantage for the employees to stay on is that the buyer will need them, and they should have continued employment. The employees should recognize the new owner not only must have them, but they will be in a strong bargaining position with the seller because the assets acquired are usually of lesser value without employees' knowledge of their operation. It is of equal importance for the seller to retain as many of his personnel as possible during the sale period to enable the buyer to acquire a going business. Any sale period is a time when rumors multiply at an unbelievable rate, and the rumors may reach a level where employees will begin to terminate unless they are properly informed and kept informed.

A candid and somewhat introspective evaluation of the personnel involved in administering and implementing the sales program must be conducted. Both the factors of availability and competence must be fully assessed. The sales program will require the time of several people described in the later chapter entitled "Organizing to Sell." An effective sales program is a time consuming matter requiring personnel with highly special skills and ability. If they are not available, less desirable alternatives including employment of consultants will have to be considered if the sales program is to progress. Bringing in outside consultants may or may not be offensive to a corporation, but it is definitely not as effective as having competent, internal personnel to carry on the program. Least effective, and worst of all for selling a subsidiary, are those operating people directly responsible for its day-to-day performance. They seldom have the time, necessary experience, or sympathy with the program, let alone enthusiasm, to be effective.

Everyone must be informed that the decision to sell is an unequivocal and final decision of the board of directors. Because of the different perspectives and personal interest of individuals involved, it is doubtful that there will be complete agreement or sympathy with the decision, but those opposed must be made aware the time for arguing is past. Everyone must realize their best interests lie in assisting in every way possible to make the sales program a success rather than spending time attempting to convince others the board decision was a mistake. The board of directors at a later date may reverse its decision or find its decision impossible to implement if the subsidiary proves unsaleable, but until such occurs everyone should understand the decision is final. A clear-cut understanding of the irreversible nature of the decision is also important to minimize conflicts between operating management and those involved in the selling program. Inherent in a sales program are conflicts between these groups; but the conflicts will be lessened if it is established that the basic objective and policy is to dispose of the subsidiary.

Former Shareholders

If the subsidiary for sale had been recently acquired by the seller, then the relationship with former shareholders or owners of the subsidiary should be reviewed. They may continue to have great status in the overall industry which cannot be ignored. If possible, relations with former shareholders should be brought to a harmonious level since they may be able to assist in the sales procedure. Wise prospects commonly contact them for their opinions since their ownership possibly included the period of time when the business was founded and went through its development stage. Former owner-managers probably recall their better decisions and believe the current owners have not distinguished themselves by displaying brilliant management. From a sales standpoint, this is not a wholly undesirable view to have presented to a prospect. Ideally, the former shareholders would be saying the current owners are people of good character, integrity, and honesty that one can bargain with, but they have not managed the subsidiary as well as the prospective buyer could easily do. Another reason for good relations with the former shareholders is that they may be prime prospects for acquiring the subsidiary. Frequently subsidiaries are purchased by their prior owners. They know the business, and believe no one can possibly run the business as well as they did and could. They have an emotional attachment to the business and may believe they could negotiate an extremely favorable deal to buy it back because of their assumed superior knowledge of the business.

Data Accuracy

The accuracy of all reports and financial statements for the subsidiary should be challenged and the seller should start with the assumption that the statements are inaccurate and hope the assumption is proven wrong. Unaudited interim operating statements of subsidiaries have a justly deserved reputation for inaccurate or misleading numbers. The inaccuracies may result from any number of factors but the major ones are ineptness, incompleteness, poor accounting systems, a manager's determination to try to make a good showing, and liberal accounting policies designed to inflate income for reporting purposes. Certain other factors may tend to present misleading results such as overhead allocations, corporate charges, inventory treatment, transfer pricing, and bad debt policies. The balance sheet should be checked to make certain it truly reflects fully the assets and liabilities of the subsidiary.

There seems to be no end to the opportunity for financial statements to become inaccurate or misleading without the occurrence of fraud or outright falsification. This problem area should be faced up to early since the seller needs readily understood, accurate statements to make intelligent decisions including the one of whether or not to sell at all. The seller can be certain a prospective buyer will not sign the closing papers until the buyer has a complete understanding of the financial statements and is convinced of their accuracy. Inaccurate statements or reports will discourage buyers through creation of suspicion of all data submitted and may even cause doubts regarding the seller's integrity. Dubious statements also bring about heavy demands for warranties, which the seller may otherwise have avoided. Should the statements be found to be inaccurate or misleading, they should be corrected and heavily footnoted to avoid any misunderstandings or charges of misrepresentation. A senior accountant should be assigned to the sales project very early to determine the accuracy of the statements while gathering or preparing the necessary data called for in Appendix A and B. Ideally, the same accountant will remain throughout the entire sales program. The accountant should become an expert on the subsidiary and be prepared to meet with accountants or other representatives of prospects and discuss the statements and accounting theories and policies utilized.

Severence Benefits

If a complete autonomous subsidiary is to be sold, then the matter of termination pay and all other employee benefits will be of less importance because the benefits and benefit obligations will continue on and become the responsibility of the new owner. However, in divestments of divisions and product lines the matter of employee benefits is one of utmost importance and frequent complexity. An early announcement of the seller's position relative to such benefits should be made to the employees and also be presented to prospective buyers to avoid any misunderstanding.

Termination pay presents a particularly difficult problem even when a subsidiary, division, or product line is being sold as a going business. Company policy statements on termination pay would be unlikely to include specific terms providing benefits in the event the operation is sold as a going business. Some employers do not even believe it wise to publish their termination pay policies, but most do. Although an employee of the operation being sold may have total continuity in employment and retain all possible benefits under the management of the new owner, the employee may feel his service was actually terminated by the prior owner and thus is entitled to separation pay.

Some United States court decisions have supported this line of reasoning, so early legal review of the applicable conditions is in order to determine the extent of liability. The seller may generously agree with the above line of reasoning, although most would not, and wish to make payment of separation pay to the employees in the operation sold. Should this course of action be chosen, it could work to the detriment of the new owner if the payments were made either at the time of closing or shortly thereafter. The new owner would rightly believe presenting the employees with a large sum of money would give them greater financial flexibility to seek employment somewhere else rather than remain. If termination pay is to be paid, then an approach where it is paid six months to a year after the closing date and contingent upon their remaining with the new owner would be more appropriate and also would be impressive to a prospective buyer.

Whatever is the policy developed by the seller on termination pay, it should be made available for early communication to the employees. A special private and supplemental termination pay bonus may be thought necessary for one or two key employees in a subsidiary that is highly dependent upon them and would be of little or no value without their services. This supplemental compensation would be an inducement to assist in the sales program and stay for a reasonable period of time with the new owner. Payment should be contingent upon remaining a minimum agreed time with the new owner and preferably not paid until the time period has elapsed. Excessive termination pay demands can also take on the nature of blackmail or extortion by unscrupulous employees who recognize their importance, and this could present the seller with a most difficult decision.

In many countries termination or severance benefits are totally determined by the government with company policies playing a minor role. Severance benefit requirements may have become so large that this is a primary cause of the divestiture with liquidation impossible but sale a way out.

Pension, Profit Sharing and Benefit Plans

Pensions and profit sharing plans must be extensively reviewed, carefully evaluated, and the resultant policy decisions communicated to employees and be available for potential prospects. These plans are designed for each specific group and are of enormous diversity and are described in boring, lengthy contracts and documents of considerable complexity. Their nature is also influenced by changing accounting policies and legislation supplemented by governmental bodies' frequent administrative rulings. Professional advice is necessary to evaluate the impact of a sale on the seller, the employees, the benefit obligations, and the assets and liabilities a buyer would be expected to assume.

It is impossible to cover here all potential problems that may surface in a comprehensive professional review, but there are several whose presence would be obvious and significant. Should the benefit plan involved be that of the parent company covering employees of the subsidiary for sale or cover employees in a division or of a product line, then the buyer must rewrite or develop a new pension or profit sharing plan and submit it to the Internal Revenue Service to secure a "letter of determination," which is in effect a letter of approval. Deletion of the employees of the subsidiary may force the seller to also reconstruct the plan and submit it to the IRS for approval. Contributed funds in the trust established for the plan created by the seller for the subsidiary's employees will not be readily transferred to any other plans, new and old, of either the buyer or seller. The subsidiary's employees' values in the existing plan of the seller will normally become 100% vested if they are in a trust where a vesting schedule applies. Under many pension or profit sharing plans 100% vesting coupled with a technical termination of the employee could result in an obligation to pay benefits due to the employees immediately after consummation of the sale. This may be the commencement of periodic benefits under a contractual program or a full lump sum settlement. An underfunded trust or one that has suffered investment reverses could be hard-pressed to come up with the cash to make the payments. Payments could deplete the funds to a point where remaining employees covered by the plan but not in the unit sold would be adversely affected. Eventually the seller may be obligated to restore the trust to sound financial condition. Buyers are usually alert to the pitfalls of pension plans and will be cautious not to assume large obligations such as unfunded past service charges. The seller should know in detail the nature of the subsidiary's plans, cost, and obligations before contacting prospects.

Great care must be taken to plan the transition of the benefit plans because of their importance to the employees and because of the substantial sums of money and potential liabilities involved. Because pension plans and profit sharing plans are part of the golden handcuffs, those benefits that lock an employee to a job, a buyer will not be anxious to seek a quick disbursement of any funds. Federal laws prevent the funds contributed to a pension or profit sharing trust from reverting back to the employer, so a seller may as well make the most of the situation for the former employees' and the buyer's benefit. These are complex and sensitive issues, and it cannot be stressed strongly enough that professional experts are needed very early to advise the seller on the ramifications of a sale.

Employees will be concerned about continuity of other existing benefits such as vacations, holidays, and insurance programs. A seller has no way to guarantee the benefits will continue unchanged under a new owner, but it can be pointed out to the employees that a new owner will need the employees and, therefore, cannot expect to inspire or retain them by reducing or eliminating benefits. Current and future vacation costs present a special problem because of the large sums involved particularly if the seller has not followed a practice of accruing costs in the year prior to which vacations are taken consistent with the theory of vacations being earned in prior years. This approach and theory associated with vacation costs is not universal but is the prevalent method with most believing such obligations should be reflected on income statements and the balance sheet. A seller who has not accrued these costs and a buyer who makes a standard practice of accruing for vacations must face up to their difference in opinions in the negotiating process. Accruals for holidays can present the same conflict but on a much smaller scale. The amount of money associated with vacation and holiday costs is substantial and cannot be ignored or sloughed over, because before a closing someone is certain to bring up the issue.

Stock purchase, stock option, and bonus plans come in many different forms, and the terms and conditions of each plan will govern the approach and influence whatever decisions are to be made relative to the respective plans. The nature of the plans are such that they must cease upon sale for the employees of the unit sold. The manner in which this is done and how it is to be communicated is a matter of great importance to the employees involved, because the employees normally would be those holding key positions. Here again is an area where professional advice may be necessary to revise the plans and propose reasonable approaches.

Benefit Plans, Funded and Unfunded

The seller's position on cash bonus, incentive, and commission plans must be carefully studied and the employees and prospective buyers should be informed in precise terms of how obligations incurred under the plans will be met. Payments for prior performance or time frames will become due in the period of new ownership and a dispute with a new owner will occur if the party liable has not been clearly identified during the negotiations. These obligations are not always accrued on financial statements as they occur, further complicating the problem. Accruing proper amounts or calculating the amount due is not a simple task as in the case of sales incentive plans based upon the total sales in a long period, such as a full year, because of fluctuations in sales volume from month to month. A new owner may hold a poor opinion of the plans and the recipients and be reluctant to pay anything unless the obligation is clearly understood and assumed. Often the incentive plans, either intentionally or inadvertently, are written with a lack of clarity and contain the opportunity for substantial management discretion. This may have worked well in the past with continuity of ownership, but it does not contribute to a stable understanding at the time of sale or under the administration of a new owner. A new owner will be wise to announce very early in the period of ownership the acceptance of the plans or ideas on revision or termination.

Obligations may exist to former employees of the subsidiary that are not fully funded and have been paid only from current funds. Group and life insurance benefits to retirees most commonly fall into this category. These are benefits awarded for long service prior to the date of the sale, and a buyer may not want to assume the obligations. Disability benefits may present a problem of the same nature. Workmen's compensation claims may present a special problem if the subsidiary was a self-insured or supplemental benefits were granted. A sales program could precipitate a large number of workmen's compensation claims because of the employees' loss of loyalty and belief that they now have nothing to lose or because they believe this may be their last chance. Special supplemental retirement benefits in the form of consulting contracts or other means of payment may have been given to long service employees who retired. Consulting contracts may have been awarded to some employees as a form of severance pay. Other employees or members of their families may have received long term scholarship awards. Who now pays these benefits must be decided.

Deferred compensation programs may be in effect for key executives. Under the terms of some plans, if an executive terminates, the amount deferred will be forfeited to the company. If the subsidiary is sold, then the executive may experience an actual or technical termination. These plans should be reviewed to ensure fair treatment of the executives. Usually the company is free to modify the plans without IRS approvals.

Internal Procedures

The seller's internal procedures for sale approval and bargaining latitude need to be clarified and understood by all involved. At some point a prospective buyer will want to be dealing with a principal representative of the seller who has the authority to make decisions necessary to conclude the negotiation. A slow, cumbersome procedure of approvals is not conducive to a successful negotiation. If the board of directors chooses to play an active role in the negotiations other than establishing general bargaining parameters, negotiations will be most difficult. The corporation in which the chief executive is all powerful and the board of director's main duty is to shout "amen" may not be the best possible approach to overseeing and managing the business, but it is an ideal arrangement for negotiating divestments. The ability to respond to changing circumstances and decisiveness are of critical importance to successfully conclude negotiations.

Another essential ingredient is that whoever is doing the negotiations, whether it is an outside attorney, a vice president, or the chief executive officer, must have access to the individual or board of directors who can make binding major decisions or be given the authority to do so. General parameters for bargaining are desirable but these must be flexible to respond to the changing circumstances that always seem to occur.

Communications

As previously mentioned, attempts to keep the divestiture secret will soon fail, and the seller should assume that once contact is made with a prospect, news of a sales possibility will spread throughout the industry, the community where the facility is located, and to all employees. Any fears the seller has of severe repercussions regarding the fact a subsidiary is for sale will probably prove to be exaggerations of what actually develops, but they should be considered. Sale programs and decisions to sell subsidiaries go on continually, and unless the transaction is very large, it will be of little interest to anyone except those individuals who are directly involved. Decisions to sell do not bring about the public relation problems a decision to liquidate or drastically curtail operations would produce. The seller should develop a truthful and accurate statement as to why the subsidiary is for sale, and this statement should be communicated to all concerned. Preferably, one company official will be responsible for making all further statements as the sales program progresses. This designated spokesperson should be the one employees or other interested parties can contact during the sales program to find out what is going on. This person also will receive calls from unsolicited prospects and should be prepared to forward these on to the appropriate party in the company for follow-up. Clandestine sales programs are impossible and unneccessary, and it is foolish to attempt to do so. The more who know of the sales program, the more prospects will learn of the opportunity and, perhaps the sooner a sale will be concluded.

Notification to the public, government, and the community where the subsidiary is located and the investment banking industry should be kept as routine as possible. The type, timing, and extent of detail will depend on the size of the assets to be sold and their importance in relation to the groups affected. A significant profit contributor or loser being placed on the market for sale would be of interest to shareholders and investment banks and could easily affect the price of the seller's shares. The subsidiary for sale that has 500 employees in a large metropolitan area would receive little or no attention whatsoever from the local media; but, if the same size subsidiary was located in a community of 10,000 to 25,000, then its availability for sale would be major news. A complete press release describing the transaction proposed should be developed and be available for release when the sale program commences. Whether anyone prints it and what portions are printed will be up to the media, usually to the chagrin of the seller. This release can be the official candid company statement for internal and external purposes. A professional public relations firm can be very helpful if the seller does not possess this capability within the organization.

Notification of customers in the industry in which the subsidiary is a part must be faced. In most cases no general notification is necessary or desirable, but the subsidiary to be sold should be prepared to give candid and truthful detailed answers to customers when they inquire as to whether or not the rumors they hear are true. (These very rumors may produce the prospect who will eventually buy the subsidiary.) Competitors will try to take advantage of the uncertainty that exists during the sales period. The best statement to customers and the one to hold the competitors at bay is to have employees of the subsidiary saying, "Yes, it is true, but we are only being sold as a business and on a basis where a new buyer must continue and improve the business. The subsidiary is not being sold on a liquidation basis, and it will be business as usual before, during, and after the sale." Employees of the subsidiary who advance strong positive statements of this type, emphasizing the continuity of the business and their intention to remain part of it, will be effective, and the seller need not be concerned that the business will appreciably deteriorate during the sales period. The business often will improve with employees staying on the job and giving greater effort in the realization that they will be eventually working for a new owner.

If the subsidiary is highly dependent upon either a small number of suppliers or customers, a program of assessing their views and reactions to a sale must be conducted. These people will in almost all cases be interested in continuing a stable relationship. There is no way to completely eliminate their fears and doubts, but a straightforward approach of informing them of the plans will help preserve the relationships. They also may even assist in finding suitable prospects or be themselves prospects.

Sensitive or Illegal Activity

A most delicate problem is that of the subsidiary that has been or presently is involved in illegal activity, which a sales program could very well expose. The seller's learning of the activity may be the very reason for the divestiture. Since failure to report a crime is a crime in itself, the seller has a severe problem that could have disastrous repercussions. Commonly, this situation may occur in the area of price fixing or planned market sharing with competitors and these violations must be stopped immediately if they do exist. The seller should question his subsidiary executives extensively on the frequency and type of contact with competitors and determine if any questionable activities exist. Political contributions, kickbacks, payoffs of various types and unusual commission arrangements may also have occurred with or without parent company knowledge and could surface in a sales program. When any activity of this nature does surface, the seller should not be too hasty in concluding what occurred was an actual violation of the law. In any case the seller will do well to issue general policy statements disapproving any illegal acts and inform all employees that such activity is against company policy and will not be tolerated and hope it will end there. The circumstances, the conscience of the company officers, and the likelihood of exposure will undoubtedly influence the seller's position if questionable activity is discovered.

The many problems associated with a subsidiary sale can usually be solved by facing up to them squarely and rationally. The seller should not forget in solving these problems that a sale is quite normal, major business decision; and there is no need for embarassment or hesitancy in proceeding. It is a business decision often involving much compassion and understanding, but it is not a moral decision.

4.
Defining
What
Is for Sale

It is not uncommon for the decision to sell to be made before having precisely defined what is to be sold. Errors in definition will nearly always be to the disadvantage of the seller, because the buyer cannot be expected to identify for the seller undervalued assets like he will undisclosed liabilities and overvalued assets. Usually at an early stage, the only thing definitely decided is that the present owner wishes to divest of a certain business and preferably by selling the business as a going concern. It would be far better to accurately define the exact nature of the subsidiary before making a final decision to sell, because certain assets, liabilities, or obligations that were not fully considered for inclusion or exclusion could not only greatly influence the price but may even show a sale to be unwise. Defining what is for sale must be done eventually so by all means do it early.

An accurate description of the subsidiary's assets and liabilities may cast doubt upon the original financial data used in making the decision and the decision itself. This would be the case if unrealistic overhead allocations were used, concealed assets or liabilities emerged or inadequate or excessive reserves were established to mention a few of the possibilities. As a part of the effort to define the subsidiary, a general program of clarifying and cleaning up the balance sheet is in order. A program of enlightenment of this type is almost certain to produce a few surprises and possibly a certain amount of embarrassment. The seller should have a complete and detailed understanding of each item on the balance sheet as well as knowledge of those assets and liabilities not represented in the financial statements. This complete information regarding each balance sheet item should be reduced to writing for ready reference. Nonbalance sheet assets, liabilities, and guarantees should also be recorded in complete detail.

It is not an easy task to define a subsidiary and may prove particularly difficult if a division or product line is the subject of a sale.

In defining what is for sale, it is also advisable to develop alternatives where certain assets or liabilities may either be included or excluded to accommodate the buyer and vary the price as could be the case when facilities may be either sold or leased to the buyer. Before prospects are contacted, it is absolutely essential to determine what is to be sold with the objective of developing a precise description of the subsidiary that can be given to prospects. A seller can easily lose as much or more money in a transaction by not knowing what he is selling as he can by improper pricing decisions.

Employee Decisions

An early question is which employees go with the sale. Will any be specifically excluded? Will some be retained by the seller or terminated if requested by the buyer prior to closing or at closing time? Will the sale be contingent upon the buyer accepting the employees for an agreed length of time? In making these decisions, the seller and buyer should not forget slavery was declared illegal long ago and an employee will only remain or go where assigned if the position is attractive. Generous termination pay, bonuses, and contractual provisions can all help encourage an employee to do as the buyer wishes but, there is no way to force the employee. In large corporations the manager of the subsidiary and one or two other employees may be all that are known to the seller's management and are consequently the only ones likely to become a subject of controversy. The people who have obvious talent or special technical skills will be very much wanted by the buyer and their employment by the buyer may become a condition of the sale. A wise buyer will also insist on contractual terms with the seller that prevent rehiring of key employees and will require the seller to do everything possible to encourage them to remain with the subsidiary. In cases where an employee provides services to both the subsidiary and to operations of the corporation not being sold, arrangements should be made for the employee to continue the services if the buyer requests or the buyer should be told very early the employee's services will not be available. Seldom is it practical for an employee to maintain a dual relationship for any length of time and it is best to plan early for the elimination of such arrangements. Subsidiaries may be serviced by a centralized research, purchasing, legal, or any other staff function that also provides services throughout the corporation. These too will have to be reviewed and sorted out for sale purposes. Important guidelines in deciding which employees are to go with the sale and which are to remain with the seller center around candidly informing the buyer early exactly who will and will not be included. Usually the buyer will want almost all the people in order to acquire a going business. At a minimum, the buyer will insist upon the key employees remaining for a fixed period of time adequate to provide an orderly transition in ownership and to find replacements if such is necessary. If a particular employee is absolutely critical to the continued success of the subsidiary's operations or an important department in the subsidiary, the seller should assume with certainty the buyer will discover this fact for himself prior to closing and insist upon the employee's tenure.

The seller should not encourage an employee to tell a buyer that he is staying with the subsidiary and then enter into a clandestine agreement to re-employ the employee after the sale. Not only are such agreements deceitful but their likely exposure can cloud the entire transaction. The seller should also guard against unauthorized subordinates, such as divisional or regional managers, making secret deals of this type.

Excluding Assets

Any assets of the subsidiary to be excluded or optional in the sale should be identified to prospective buyers in the first sales presentation to avoid misunderstanding. In this category could be real estate that could be retained by the seller and leased for a period of time to the buyer or investments of the subsidiary in unrelated businesses or marketable securities. Automobiles, airplanes, or recreational facilities possibly may be excluded and any other tangible assets may be considered. Withholding of select assets not essential to the business or those candidates for lease arrangements are means of reducing the price to a level acceptable or possible for a buyer. Assets whose present market value is less than book value may also be withheld to delay or avoid write-offs in the seller's financial reports. Assets that are greatly undervalued should be considered for exclusion from the transaction unless their presence is reflected in the price. Frequently, real estate is stated on the books at a value far less than market. Sometimes it is advantageous to sell the business at a low price with the provision that it be moved so that the real estate can be sold separately.

Surplus, excess, and superfluous assets such as scrap, old or unused machines, real estate, investments, excess inventory, vehicles or aircraft can frequently be sold separately prior to a sale without adversely affecting the probability or price of the subsidiary sale. The seller should check for little known assets acquired as a result of foreclosures or defaulted collateral received when customers failed to pay. Any assets that are totally unrelated to the conduct of the business should be considered for exclusion. Surplus assets will bring little or nothing extra in price in the total subsidiary sale and their prior disposition may actually help the appearance of the subsidiary and consequently the sale. Disposal of excess assets of this type undoubtedly should have been going on in the normal course of business but, in all probability, this has not been the case and a special program under the direction of strong-willed management will be necessary to dispose of the assets. Assets needed in the business definitely should not be sold and the seller should avoid removing essential assets on the assumption a new owner will never miss what was never seen. Sales of needed assets will be resented by potential buyers and their absence will create distrust and possibly jeopardize the sale.

Receivables

A major item for inclusion or exclusion and an area that will be fully negotiated before closing occurs is receivables. Seldom are receivables 100% collectible, so it is common for all or part of the receivables to either be excluded from the sale or discounted. Written-off receivables should be excluded because they will add nothing to the price and there is a small chance someday they may be collected. Establishment of reserves or guarantees on the collectibility of receivables is a common means of handling assurances that the receivables are collectible and this may prove to be the most reasonable approach. Total or partial exclusion eliminates any doubt as to their value to the business and it also is a major method for reducing the immediate price to the buyer.

Exclusion eliminates for the seller the opportunity to pass on to the buyer receivables of a questionable nature, although this may be contrary to one of the objectives of the seller. If excluded receivables are readily collectible, then it will add immediate cash to the transaction for the seller. However, a seller who sells receivables or retains the receivables will have to rely to some degree upon the buyer for their collection. The seller will not have, under normal circumstances after the sale, the personnel or the paperwork systems to handle the collections. A buyer may also be reluctant to have the seller become involved in collections for fear of jeopardizing relations with the customers. A ruthless collection approach on the part of the former owner could adversely affect customer relations.

Inventory

Inventory is another category of assets that may provide an opportunity for exclusion. The true value of inventory is always an area for controversy and any excluded automatically eliminates or reduces the area of controversy. Excess raw material or finished products that are readily marketable may possibly be excluded. A company that had followed an aggressive policy of writing off questionable and slow moving inventory to temporarily reduce tax liabilities may wish to exclude some of this "worthless" inventory. If it is not excluded, it should be reflected in the price received for the subsidiary but this will be difficult. It will take considerable persuasive selling to convince a buyer written-off inventory is of value. The book value of the inventory should be equated against current market value and if a substantial difference exists, then the seller should consider alternate methods of reflecting true value either prior to or at time of sale. If market value is under book value, then nothing can be done other than the unpleasant action of writing down the inventory. However, it would take an obvious situation to induce most sellers to write down their inventory prior to sale. An undervalued inventory's true value could be reflected on financial statements with explanatory footnotes or in forecasts showing the effect on profits when it is sold. Whenever the seller believes the inventory to be undervalued and chooses to make an issue of the fact, the seller should be fully prepared to defend the position because such claims will be treated skeptically by prospects.

Cash

The cash of the subsidiary may be kept in a parent company bank account or in an account controlled by the subsidiary. In any business the cash will fluctuate up and down with the daily requirements and success of the business. The cash account can vary hour by hour making a policy and negotiating position absolutely essential. A cash flow forecast will be helpful in arriving at a decision on negotiating position, but such forecasts can only be treated as unreliable guides for a point in time many months away. Divisional and product line sales will almost of necessity be a sale of selected assets and liabilities and logically any cash assets will be excluded from the transaction and retained by the seller. In the case of a full corporate subsidiary being sold that utilizes the cash management services of the parent with the parent in possession of the cash, the problem is more complex.

There is no one best way to handle the cash asset in a sales program that is applicable to all situations and conditions. In most cases the seller will have to evaluate all factors and make a decision. The decision could include allowing all cash to go with the transaction, allowing no cash to be included, or agreeing on some fixed amount of cash to be included.

Engineering companies and manufacturers of capital equipment attempt to negotiate as large as possible mobilization payments or down payments with receipt of order and subsequent progress payments. Should the subsidiary be involved in receiving such payments, then the seller must carefully determine his bargaining position and decide what cash goes with the sale. Exceptionally accurate financial statements are necessary to match jobs costs against cash received to determine the true conditions. This is not an easy task even for competent professionals with the most honest of intentions because of the difficulty in determining the exact status of jobs in progress. Controversies over what are proper interim profit pick-ups and the ultimate amount of retentions will further complicate matters. The seller should not only review his position considering the current condition of the company, but also what would happen if a large advance or progress payment was received a few days before closing. Retention of all the cash by the seller is usually unrealistic if the subsidiary has in its possession cash advances from customers for work to be performed.

Excluding Liabilities

Not only may a seller exclude specific assets from a transaction, but he may decide it is advisable to exclude specific liabilities in order to make the transaction more attractive. Jobs or projects not fully completed and still in progress may contain losses or their outcome is so uncertain that they must either be excluded from the transaction or the seller must agree to reimburse the buyer for whatever ultimate losses result. In addition to loss jobs any liability is a candidate for exclusion with indebtedness to the parent or sister subsidiaries, bank debt, and income taxes as other prime possibilities. When the financial results of a subsidiary have been consolidated with the parent company for tax purposes, any outstanding tax liability of the subsidiary that is actually a liability of the parent, must be evaluated and given special attention in deciding to include or exclude, and if included determine how it will be paid. The complexity of the tax problem when a sale occurs in the middle of a tax year for subsidiaries whose parents file consolidated returns is severe and expert assistance will be required. Further complicating the problem is that the tax booked by a consolidated subsidiary may be very different from that actually paid by the parent. With liabilities of any type it may not be the seller's option to decide if they will be excluded or included but the decision may rest with creditors, customers, or those guaranteed.

Splitting a Subsidiary

Subsidiaries with multiple locations should be reviewed with the possibility of breaking up and selling each location individually. The disadvantages of multiple sales are that there are multiple costs and sales programs involved for each sale, but the disadvantages may be offset by advantages and necessity. In some cases the subsidiary is so large it can only be sold if broken up. Retention of some locations is also an alternate to consider. It may be possible a subsidiary would lend itself to this type of program and the combined price for the individual parts would be greater than the price anticipated if sold as a complete package. Certain locations of the subsidiary may be unprofitable or marginal and it could be more advantageous to liquidate the losing operations and then sell or retain the balance of the viable locations. Prospective buyers are seldom anxious to take on the job of liquidating any part of the business unless they only are paying a liquidation price. Physical assets of some locations may be of more value to the seller if retained and transferred to operations not for sale. It may be possible to combine the inventory of two locations into one making a more saleable business. The potential variations of partial sales, retentions, and liquidations is endless but whatever is practical should not be too difficult to identify and evaluate in each situation.

Service and Warranty

The responsibility for service and product warranty will be a critical point in the negotiations and accounting and technical assistance will be needed to develop an intelligent position. The recent large, well publicized settlements of law suits involving warranty issues, product liability, and the frequency of spurious and fraudulent claims has made everyone in business wary. The first step is for a seller to determine how much probable warranty exposure, if any, exists. A review of prior years warranty expenses will give some indication but interrogation of subsidiary management, sales, engineering, and manufacturing personnel as to the present level of claims and potential claims is necessary. The complexity of this problem and the difficulty of solution should not be underestimated and the seller should determine early a preferred and realistic position.

A buyer will be reluctant to take on unlimited and unknown warranty obligations for equipment and services sold prior to the date of closing. Once the subsidiary is sold, the seller will no longer be in a position to have personnel available to evaluate warranty claims, manufacture parts, or make the necessary repairs. The seller will have to rely upon the buyer for this service and the buyer will expect to be compensated. Potential claims for work in progress is also an area for dispute, because a buyer can argue defects occurred before closing. A buyer will be desirous of maintaining excellent relations with the customers and will not wish to see a nonconciliatory approach towards warranty claims as easily could happen if the seller retained full financial responsibility for all warranties but had no interest in continuing customer relations.

The seller will desire to minimize warranty expenses and be suspicious that the buyer will charge an exorbitant amount to correct warranty problems. Solutions to all of these issues exist and usually in the form of carefully constructed compromises, but the level and nature of the problem will first have to be discerned. Knowledge of the extent of the problem will keep the negotiations on a realistic basis rather than wild speculation about all the things that could go wrong but never have. The parties should agree in complete detail in their negotiations as to how these issues will be resolved on the valid assumption that it will be easier in the negotiations than in the courthouse months later. Neither the buyer nor seller should attempt to slip by this issue in early negotiations since it is certain to surface during negotiations of the definitive agreement.

Patents and Trademarks

Patents, licensing, or franchise agreements may be critical assets for the subsidiary and without them the subsidiary would be of little value. Some corporations have complex internal structures set up primarily for tax reasons whereby the parent company or one special subsidiary of the parent company owns all patents for the corporation with each subsidiary paying royalties to the patent holder. Agreements may also be applicable to operations of the seller other than the subsidiary to be sold. Retention of patents and licensing agreements by the seller is a convenient means of reducing the initial price. The buyer, through the device of making royalty payments over a period of time from the pre-tax revenues of the subsidiary acquired, could find this approach to be a very attractive means of paying for the subsidiary out of cash generated by the subsidiary.

Trade names and trademarks utilized by the subsidiary exclusively should present no problem. However, if they are applicable to other subsidiaries and the parent company in general, then a clear agreement on the utilization of the trademarks must be developed. In cases where the seller will retain ownership and continue to use the name or trademark, an orderly transition must be permitted the buyer. A reasonable approach is where the buyer for an agreed period of time would be permitted to indicate on the product, advertising material, and product literature the former trademark and name but also phase in a new name and trademark. In some transactions, the transition will be long, difficult, and expensive.

Insurance

The nature of the insurance coverage for the subsidiary should be considered. There will be little difficulty if conventional insurance is in effect where for a fixed premium, coverage is provided and the subsidiary does not have an unusual loss experience. However, if the subsidiary is self-insured, included in other overall corporate plans, insured on some sort of retrospective basis, or has an extremely poor loss experience, then careful planning and establishment of a detailed bargaining position will be required. Each category of insurance protection, fire, workmen's compensation, group, general liability, and product liability must be reviewed. If self-insurance exists, then the new owner will have to find a carrier to take over. The seller can also expect to experience an abnormal surge of group insurance and workmen's compensation claims once news of the subsidiary's possible sale is common knowledge. Coverage in overall corporate programs will have to cease once the subsidiary is sold. If plans exist where premiums are rebated when loss experience is favorable, then it must be decided who receives the rebates. The loss experience of the subsidiary and the overall quality of the buyer will determine how readily the buyer can find a carrier to provide coverage. The deletion of the subsidiary's insurance from the seller's complete insurance program could have a significant effect upon the seller if the subsidiary had either a very bad or very good loss experience or the premiums of the subsidiary represented a major portion of the total premiums.

Expense Items

Any business purchases on a current expense basis, various supplies, such as stationery, fuel, perishable tools, and advertising or sales promotion material. These items are treated as a current expense because they will be readily consumed and they are of relatively low value. A search should be made to make certain this is actually the case. On occasion an abnormal supply may be acquired because of some special condition. A particularly advantageous price may have been offered, an entire season's fuel supply may have been purchased or possibly a large quantity of advertising material or catalogs were recently acquired. When abnormal supplies of material that are normally expensed exists, then it is reasonable to attach notes to the financial statements to reflect this condition. Unless this step is taken or some other move is made to highlight this condition, the seller will receive no credit in the sale because they will not appear on the balance sheet. The seller also would show depressed earnings during the period the material was paid for and this could adversely affect the seller's bargaining arguments and price justification.

Litigation

Litigation or potential litigation either by or against the subsidiary must be assessed. A buyer will only with great reluctance take on uninsured liabilities of an unknown nature or pay for intangible assets whose value is yet to be determined. Therefore, the cost of unfavorable litigation or results of favorable litigation will of necessity remain with the seller if the potential outcome could be a significant amount. Minor routine litigation can go with the subsidiary but even in those cases, a buyer will normally want protection from unlimited liability by the seller when such is not already covered by insurance. Litigation remaining with the seller may require the services of the employees of the buyer and in such cases, the cost of their services should be a subject of negotiations in the purchase agreement.

Accruals and Reserves

Accruals, reserves, and retentions may appear on a balance sheet covering any conceivable number of items. A seller should develop a list of all such items and evaluate each and make decisions as to how they will be treated. Those found to be unrealistic should be promptly adjusted to make the balance sheet reflect the true condition of the subsidiary prior to contact of prospects. Reserves at times tend to accumulate on a balance sheet although the reason for their establishment has long since passed. Reserves and accruals should be given special review for adequacy because these may be understated for any number of reasons including lack of information, uncertainty as to amounts, acounting policies, and, possibly, a desire to prop up income. Accruals for compensation and fringe benefit costs such as vacations, holidays, retirement benefits, commissions, and profit sharing should be given special attention. The obvious reserve categories for bad debts and inventory obsolescence will receive ample attention before any transaction is consummated. The seller will expose problems in the subsidiary through establishment of reserves, but these can be presented in a more palatable form by the seller rather than in a belated explanation when the problems are discovered in a buyer's investigation and audit. Retentions are amounts withheld by customers until work by a subsidiary has been performed to the satisfaction of the customer or released under terms of a contract. When retentions exist, each will have to be examined as to collectability.

Assets and Liabilities
Not on the Financial Statements

After the careful evaluation of all balance sheet items for inclusion or exclusion decisions, a search for other assets that normally would not be shown as balance sheet items should be conducted. The major item in a manufacturing or engineering operation is the status of the backlog. A large order backlog of profitable work could be the most important asset of all. A very small backlog could at a minimum be a danger signal to prospects and a backlog with low margin or loss jobs could be an actual liability. To make the subsidiary saleable, loss jobs may have to be removed from the sale or a guarantee given to the buyer to ensure against unreasonable losses. The overall amount and condition of the backlog will play a major role in pricing. Significant new products from the subsidiary's research and development program may soon be ready for production. The value of such developments are difficult to assess but an aggressive seller will not understate their potential. The seller may even wish to exclude key developments from the sale. Long-term leases may have a value far greater than expected because of inflation or other factors. These too need evaluation. Backlog, R & D developments, and leases are the common unrecorded assets but a seller should not limit the search to them. The seller should systematically review all categories of items purchased that were expensed and not capitalized to see if any unusual values exist.

If the business is a division or product line and not a subsidiary, then a review is worthwhile to determine if it could easily be restructured into a complete business in corporation form. If the transformation is not readily accomplished then it will not be worth the effort unless a prospect has made this a requirement of the sale. A complete, going business will be attractive to more prospective buyers than a division or product line with missing departments and personnel. There is more demand for complete businesses and negotiations for complete businesses are more easily accomplished. If a complete subsidiary is not created, the missing parts must be clearly enumerated for business evaluation, pricing purposes, and the buyer. Missing departments are not always a detriment to a sale because the buyer may already have such departments or prefer to create them. Should the sale be contingent upon moving the business and integrating it with existing operations of the buyer, then missing departments may cause no difficulty at all.

Defining what is for sale may prove to be relatively simple or extraordinarily difficult, but a seller will be wise to assume that it is difficult. Determination of exactly what is for sale or what are the possibilities for inclusion and exclusion of assets and liabilities is a necessary prerequisite for determining the structure of a transaction and the price.

5.
Pricing

Rational price setting is neither an art nor a science but a highly subjective exercise conducted within a general framework largely determined by market forces. There are no universally accepted formulas or standards that will permit a seller to readily calculate the "right" price, but an understanding of the mélange of factors to be evaluated will enable the seller to set a defensible and convincing price.

Numerous factors affect price, and the weight assigned to each factor varies greatly with the given situation, the time of the transaction, and the opinions and judgment of the participants. The seller will select and emphasize the factors that appear convincing to prospective buyers and support the asking price. A prospective buyer will listen carefully with little comment on the acceptable factors, challenge those with which he disagrees, and stress those he believes will justify a lower price. Key factors of book value, appraised value, liquidation values, order backlog, earnings history, earning expectations, new capital needs, market size, what the seller requires to make the sale attractive to him, growth prospects for the subsidiary, the conceptual future business plan, and the overall psychology of the situation all combine with varying degrees of emphasis to determine what a buyer will pay based upon the buyer's belief that a particular price will bring a satisfactory return on the investment. Regardless of the seller's price requirements, internal political problems, egotistical views of his selling and negotiating skills, and the buyer's lack of same, if the prospect does not become convinced that a reasonable return on the investment is inevitable, the prospect will not buy and the seller's position and arguments are meaningless. The prospect's assumptions and estimates of what can be done with the subsidiary may be cockeyed or may be voided by subsequent events, but at the time of sale, the prospect must harbor few doubts about the wisdom of his decision and the projected return.

Pricing should be such that the seller will not be getting back the subsidiary as could be the case if an unrealistic price and terms were extracted from a financially weak buyer. The seller's terms and price should enable the buyer to succeed; and, if the seller demands a price or terms that the subsidiary will not support, then the seller knows the price is too great. Capable buyers can calculate too and will come to the same conclusion and back away when they find debt service exceeds earning expectations. The seller cannot take the attitude how a buyer pays for the subsidiary is exclusively the buyer's problem.

However, before a realistic price can be set, certain basic information must be secured; and it must be resolved how the transaction is to be structured and precisely what will be included and excluded from the transaction. There are numerous ways the sale of a subsidiary can be structured, ranging from a sale of stock including all assets and liabilities to a sale of selected assets and liabilities with variations on payment terms limited only by the imagination of the participants.

Structuring the Sale

Sales of divisions and product lines that are not complete corporate subsidiaries will be structured on the basis of being a sale of selected assets and liabilities. While it may be possible, it usually will be difficult and unnecessary, unless the seller hopes to retain a minority equity interest, to incorporate a division or product line and structure the transaction on a stock sale basis. The sale of an existing subsidiary may be structured either as a sale of stock or a sale of assets and liabilities. The decisions that were made in determining exactly what was to be included and excluded from the sale can be accommodated in either a stock sale or a sale of assets type transaction. A buyer may feel more comfortable when buying only identified, selected assets and liabilities, but the actual result can be made identical to that of a sale of the stock of a total subsidiary. Every seller will prefer to sell a business on a "where is, as is" basis and let the buyer take on all known and unknown liabilities but assumption of undefined risks calls for a very reduced price, and it is unlikely that a buyer would accept at any price a subsidiary on this basis.

Equally possible is a sale of stock with a combination of warranties, representations, and designated asset and liability exclusions that is equivalent to a typical sale of assets. A sale of selected assets and liabilities can prove to be a complicated and cumbersome transaction because all major items must be identified and specifically listed. Oversights or inadvertant exclusions from the lists can work to the detriment of either party or may not adequately convey their intent. If certain assets or liabilities, which are legally owned by the subsidiary, are to be excluded from the sale, then the ownership of the excluded assets or obligations must be conveyed to another corporate entity of the current owner. This should be accomplished as soon as the decision to sell with the assets excluded is made. The seller should not wait until the last minute before closing, because everyone has enough to do just before closing without spending time on matters that could easily have been done previously.

There is no one best way to structure a sale because the facts of each situation and the prejudices of the participants must be accommodated. The seller should remain flexible as to structure but determine initially the optimum approach to structuring the transaction in order to establish a price. Other structures can represent fallback positions and concessions during the bargaining process with or without the same result. An imaginative approach to structuring that attracts and solves problems for potential buyers can be the key to a successful divestiture program, particularly when the subsidiary is presently in a loss position.

Sale of the business and limited, select assets is a common technique for reducing the price to a level the buyer can afford and eliminating disputed items from the transaction. A prospective buyer's attorney will usually be quick to recommend purchasing on a sale of assets basis because it simplifies keeping known and unknown liabilities with the seller. Retention by the seller of receivables, inventories, warranty responsibility and the like tends to eliminate controversy at time of sale and will reduce the buyer's initial cash outlay. However, a business cannot survive unless essential assets are all or partially replaced by the buyer within a short time after the purchase so deletions may not appreciably reduce a buyer's total investment. This approach is attractive to prospects with established lines of credit for working capital who may also have restrictions either self-imposed or by creditors on the amounts they can spend on acquisitions. Usually the seller's best bargaining position is to sell the complete subsidiary with all assets and liabilities and not volunteer exclusion of specific items until it becomes certain the exclusions are necessary to accommodate the buyer either by eliminating problem areas or reducing the price. Candidates for exclusion will surface when the parties are negotiating the representation and warranties provisions of their definitive contract, and contract provisions calling for outright exclusion may be the only way agreement can be reached.

Price to Reflect Changes

The condition of any company changes day to day thus creating something of a moving target for pricing purposes. Profits and losses occur, inventories fluctuate, receivables are collected or turn bad, obligations are reduced or increased only to mention a few of the possibilities. A cash flow forecast for the subsidiary that reveals either a large inflow of cash or shortage of cash immediately before or after closing must be taken into consideration when setting the price. Since months will elapse between the time of first disclosing a price and the actual closing, it is desirable to make the price a function of the condition of the company at the time of closing. The common approach is to vary the price with the net worth at closing or guarantee the net worth will be a certain minimum amount. Increases in net worth can be controlled by dividends or other appropriate parent company charges. The actual net worth cannot be accurately determined until after the closing occurs when the seller will be at a disadvantage with respect to closing the books and making the net worth calculation. The seller will no longer be in possession of the subsidiary or the complete financial records, and it will then be the buyer's personnel who determine the net worth. In the absence of clear guidelines, this could be a great opportunity for an unscrupulous or suddenly disenchanted buyer.

Accounting approaches and principles do vary, making it essential for the definitive contract of the sale of the business to include very exact guidelines specifying how net worth will be determined and designating a specific public accounting firm to audit the calculations. If inventory is included in the transaction, extreme care should be taken to precisely define the method of valuation unless one or both parties wants a deal so badly they are willing to argue over inventory value after the closing. It is fair to both parties if the price has variable features that will reflect changes in the condition of the company during the interim periods between first contact, preliminary agreement, and closing.

Necessary Preliminary Data

Prior to finalizing the pricing approach, the entire contemplated transaction must be studied from a tax viewpoint to determine the ramifications for the seller and any potential advantages for a buyer. Most buyers will want to structure the transaction in such a way as to minimize current taxes and increase cash flow, but in some public companies the emphasis is on reportable current income rather than cash flow. The seller should determine the buyer's tax approach early to facilitate structuring the transaction on an attractive basis. The buyer's main tax interest is usually to have as high a portion of the purchase price as possible assigned to depreciable assets. This may not be desirable from the seller's position, and compromises will be necessary. Buyers will be looking for other advantages such as tax loss credits and those provided by investment tax credits if the buyer has other income.

Divestitures in most cases are for cash and notes, but occasionally stock is used, particularly in situations where the transaction is extremely large or the seller is very anxious to conclude a sale. Each type of currency or combination thereof has its own tax implications. The seller's overall corporate tax position must be reviewed and the advantages and disadvantages of all cash versus installment sales or stock weighed.

The timing of receipts from the sale in relation to other income or losses within the corporation is another critical factor. If stock is received in exchange for stock of the subsidiary, then the present tax implications, as well as the tax effect when the stock is eventually sold, must be evaluated. It is unusual for a company receiving stock in a divestiture to be interested in long-term retention of the stock, thus marketability becomes important. Timing as to receipt of cash and date for payment of taxes on the cash must also be considered. A wholly owned subsidiary to be divested that has been consolidated with the parent for tax purposes but reflects on its books a substantial unpaid current tax obligation should be given special consideration when establishing the price to clearly define who will actually pay the booked tax obligation. Goodwill acquired by the buyer has its tax implications, and the buyer will also be required to write it off over a period of time. Provisions preventing the seller from competing with the business sold may be assigned a reasonable value and be depreciated by the buyer. Such "non-compete" clauses can be very advantageous to the buyer and are normally relatively meaningless for the seller, but they do have tax implications for both. Even the location of the closing and contract signing may have tax importance to avoid or reduce local, state, or federal taxes. It may be advisable to have the closing in another country or create an offshore company to receive profits or losses from the sale. A subsidiary presently consolidated with its parent may be removed from the consolidated returns of the parent by "selling" it to a foreign-based subsidiary of the parent. This makes all or part of the subsidiary's tax loss credits transferable with the sale and usable by the eventual buyer. Tax advice for subsidiary sales should be sought only from experts experienced in such transactions because of their complexity and the valuable assistance the experts can provide.

Break-Even Points

The seller should know the true break-even points before pricing the subsidiary. One break-even point will be the amount that must be received net after taxes in order to have neither a gain nor a loss, under the assumption the subsidiary is sold instantly without any changes. The seller also should make a supplemental calculation of break-even net after taxes that includes anticipated losses or gains during the sales period and all estimated costs to complete the sale. Both may prove to be more complicated calculations than the seller anticipates with the results quite a surprise. The seller who expects to price the subsidiary substantially above what is believed to be the break-even point may consider the calculations unnecessary, but early pricing hopes are often subject to modifications as the sales program and negotiations progress. If the seller expects to sell at a loss, then it is necessary to know the extent of the anticipated loss and set up reserves to cover such losses. Reserves will properly be established at the time the decision is made to sell at a loss. Public companies in particular will find timing of losses a critical management decision because they will have to disclose any material reserves established and under certain conditions publicly announce if they are classifying the subsidiary as a discontinued operation. Public disclosures give a sophisticated prospect insight into the seller's bargaining position and tend to negate certain price arguments because a prospect may believe any amounts written off are not expected to be recovered in the sale by the seller.

The seller needs to know the true book value of the subsidiary. The book value as reflected on a subsidiary balance sheet may not necessarily represent the corporation's actual book value. In cases where the subsidiary was acquired by an exchange of stock and the value of the stock exceeded the net worth of the company acquired at the time of acquisition, the book value could be misleading if the resultant goodwill is carried in parent company accounts rather than the subsidiary's.

In acquisitions involving tax-free exchanges of stock, the subsidiary acquired retains as a base for tax calculation purposes the value invested by the original shareholders, further complicating a determination of the book value and break-even points. A careful review to ascertain that the balance sheet of the subsidiary accurately reflects the assets and liabilities of the subsidiary to be sold is particularly important in calculations of break-even points. Through accounting errors or simultaneous use of assets by several subsidiaries, book value could be inaccurate. Discretionary policies involving depreciation schedules, corporate charges, or expensing of items that could have been capitalized or included in inventory also must be taken into account.

A thorough understanding of the true book value and any stated book value of a subsidiary is not only important in determining pricing, but it is necessary knowledge for the negotiating process. A buyer will be looking at book value as the break-even point and possible minimum objective for the seller (although it may not be) and book value as the amount that can be safely taken onto the balance sheet without acquiring goodwill. A book value price is a common objective for either a buyer or a seller, but should only be offered by a seller when supported by return on investment calculations. There is no reason to sell at book value just because it is a convenient bench mark number. While book value may be totally unrelated to present liquidation value or future earning expectations, it all too commonly becomes an artificial standard under which the divestiture activity is judged. If the subsidiary is sold for more than book value, it is considered a good divestiture and if sold for less, a bad one. Sellers should avoid this unrealistic standard because businesses sold at book value may be sold many times below their real value and others sold at book value or below could represent a great accomplishment for the seller.

Liquidation and Appraised Values

Liquidation values constitute a rock bottom price level and should be estimated so the seller is always aware of the probable results of this alternative. Prospective buyers may request this information to facilitate calculating their maximum loss if everything goes wrong for them. Liquidation value is not easy to calculate and will never be known exactly until one attempts a liquidation, but a reasonable estimate is important data to have available. A high liquidation value is a powerful selling point, and a low liquidation value is a point the seller will be wise not to mention. In conjuction with an estimated total liquidation value, it is helpful to have estimated market values of the individual major assets.

In cases of very large pieces of real estate where the seller is certain of the outcome, it may be worthwhile to have a formal appraisal conducted that could be presented to prospective buyers to support price requirements. If the results of an appraisal are uncertain, the seller will be better off without one, and thus avoid having to conceal or disclose unfavorable values. Most sophisticated buyers are justly suspicious of any appraisals because of their subjective nature and the differences of opinion that can exist between appraisers. It is also known that some appraisers are far more reputable than others. Regardless, it is worthwhile to have appraisals handy if they were previously constructed for other uses or are not too expensive and their contents do not hurt the seller's position. A substitute for appraisals are replacement cost estimates that are usually easy to obtain and can be secured by the seller personally. As a result of inflation, long lead times, and delivery or construction schedules, replacement comparisons can prove to be very impressive. Even with substantial discounts for wear or reduced future life, which will be a subjective exercise, the replacement values determined can effectively support a seller's pricing arguments.

Flexibility in Pricing

Finally, after it has been decided exactly what is for sale, the necessary financial data has been gathered and a decision has been made on how the sale is to be structured, a price can be established. It is best to set a fixed, realistic cash price which can be rationalized and justified to prospective buyers, and this price should be maintained throughout or until very near the end of final negotiations. The cash price should be specified in the currency of the seller's choice if the transaction is international in nature. Ridiculously large prices for bargaining purposes should be avoided because they create doubt regarding the intelligence, credibility, and integrity of the seller, and they tend to scare off prospective buyers.

Some flexibility in price in final negotiations usually becomes a psychological necessity, but these concessions should not be of a magnitude whereby they cast doubt on the original price rationale and the integrity of the seller. The final bargaining latitude need not be established until price negotiations are about to commence and early decisions should be subject to last minute review. The seller should avoid totally rigid bargaining positions and recognize the practical and psychological necessity of some flexibility, but this flexibility should not be displayed until serious negotiations commence which appear to have a good chance of producing agreement. Firm stands on price and terms are always easier for those who are not at the bargaining table, but rigid positions do not readily lead to signed contracts.

The seller must be able to justify the price with logical arguments showing how the buyer will realize an excellent return on the investment. Otherwise, the seller is in a position of saying "take it or leave it" and this is an offensive position that will not encourage a good atmosphere in a complex negotiation. An unsupported "take it or leave it" pricing policy will probably mean there are no negotiations unless the unlikely condition exists where the buyer already knows more about the subsidiary than the seller and believes the price to be a bargain. If the seller is reluctant to sell because of an ambivalent policy, rapid improvement in the fortunes of the subsidiary, or because the seller had no plans to sell but decided to consider upon being approached, unsolicited, by a buyer, then a fixed high price supported only by the rationale of "this is what we would take" is sensible. However, this approach is not conducive to bringing about a sale.

A fixed realistic price is essential for presentation to and negotiating with multiple prospects because each prospect cannot be quoted a different price. A seller can assume the price discussions with any particular prospect will become common knowledge. The lowest price quoted at any stage of negotiations with a particular prospect can easily become the new asking price and starting point in negotiations with a different prospect. An auction or bidding approach is almost impossible because of the complexity of the transactions and difficulty in securing legally binding bids. The time between oral agreements, non-binding letters of intent, and the signing of a definitive agreement, plus the multitude of legal excuses a disillusioned prospective buyer can find not to go ahead with a transaction precludes an auction approach. It is also unlikely a seller will be blessed with many prospects all clamoring to buy at once.

Negotiating Terms

There usually is far more opportunity to negotiate terms than price, and terms can prove to be of greater importance than price. Focusing the negotiations on terms tends to bring about a tacit agreement over price. However, a seller will be wise not to volunteer broad terms in detail when informing a prospect of the price. Terms and their unlimited variations will soon enough occupy the time of the negotiators. The seller should strive to keep the terms and transaction simple. A good principle to remember is that the more complicated a deal becomes, the less chance there is of it being consummated. It is all too easy for imaginative negotiators to evolve hopelessly complex terms in their desire to accommodate each other's problems, but complicated transactions have many disadvantages. They are not readily understood; there are more points for arguments; they create unnecessary suspicions; they require prolonged negotiations that again are undesirable and have lower chance of success.

Price-Earning (PE) Ratios

In setting a price, price-earning ratios should not be a major factor, and it is best to avoid PE ratios in the price setting discussions. If the subsidiary is in a loss position, then PE ratios must absolutely be avoided. In negotiations with prospective buyers, PE ratios may cautiously be used to provide peripheral support to basic negotiating positions; but a seller cannot stress them too strongly without running the risk of being trapped with an unsound position.

PE ratios have little value in pricing for a number of reasons. There never has been universally accepted agreement as to what is a fair PE ratio, and any trend toward consensus in this matter varies from time to time and from industry to industry. For calculation purposes, the earnings base may be current earnings, a five-year average, a three-year average, last year's earnings, or even a projection for the future. The consideration used in transactions is not standard, and any PE ratio where the consideration is cash would justly be much lower than where the consideration is a high multiple, difficult to market, common stock paying little or no dividend. Arguments over PE ratios are generally useless because the participants are seldom talking about the same thing because of the absence of agreed definitions.

Present Value Pricing

Another approach to price is to calculate the present market value of future earnings. With this method, future earnings are forecast for a given number of years and then mathematically discounted to theoretical present value with the price being the sum of each year's discounted earnings. This is an exercise enjoyed by financial intellectuals but not worth the time unless a buyer absolutely insists upon such calculations. A seller should not volunteer a price based on this approach since it has as many areas for argument as PE calculations. It is based on a forecast that must be open to debate itself, and unless the earnings are agreed upon, the calculations leading to price are meaningless. Even if earnings forecasts are noncontroversial, there is no agreed standard of how many future years earnings should be included. There also is no universally accepted percentage factor consistent from year to year that could be used to calculate today's value of futu e earnings, which may or may not occur. It is a rather esoteric approach that should be avoided unless a buyer is absolutely determined to use it. The odds are that if used, it will not work to the buyer's advantage because the buyer would have to accept a forecast and standards of calculation. The seller would have the advantage of first making the calculation and seeing the result before accepting this method of price determination.

The Conceptual Business Plan

Past earnings records of the subsidiary will be of great interest because they are known and tend to be indicators of the future. They are unreliable prophets, but they are tangible, available, and will receive greater attention than other items. The seller should be prepared for such discussions and be able to explain good or bad performance. Past earnings records are helpful in justifying purchase decisions to the buyer's shareholders and directors. Prior earnings are important, but a far more important factor is what are the probable future earnings. Only future anticipated earnings can justify a particular price and ultimately prove the fairness of the price. The size and condition of the backlog in a manufacturing or engineering company will be the best indication of the financial results to be anticipated short-term. The estimated future total market and competitive position will be the best long-term guide for all businesses.

The entire process of setting a price must center around a review of all pertinent factors and the development of an earnings forecast that supports a price readily and conclusively demonstrating a buyer will receive a superior return on an investment. A conceptual business plan for the successful operation of the subsidiary will be the basis for the forecast, the resultant price, and the sales presentation as described in the later chapter, "Developing a Sales Program." The conceptual business plan for the subsidiary that the seller must conceive for pricing and sales presentations should be a five-year plan prepared on a basis that is neither conservative nor unrealistic, but highly probable if specific events occur and actions are taken. It should show improvement each year. The plan should be so carefully and thoughtfully developed that it could be a viable alternative for the seller if the subsidiary is not sold and is so convincing that loyal members of the selling team come to believe the subsidiary should not be sold or at a minimum, it is most unfortunate it must be sold.

The plan's concepts and results will be reviewed, analyzed, and criticized by prospects who are sophisticated and knowledgeable in the industry and have the capability to spot fallacies that will be detrimental to the seller's position. Therefore, the most able members of the seller's management, the subsidiary's management, and others available with strong business ability should be enlisted to aid in conceiving the concepts for maximizing the subsidiary's plan performance. The seller will be wise to have several plans developed independently and then extract the best features of each to finalize on the rationale. The seller should not have either all operating personnel or all financial personnel develop the plan but secure the participation of both.

The major assumptions of the plan should not be controversial and the operational concepts readily seen as obvious moves that can easily be accomplished by the buyer. This is all the more important when the subsidiary is unprofitable or only marginal as is usually the case. Those preparing the plan must have or acquire a complete knowledge of the subsidiary and its markets including a comprehensive list of the subsidiary's weak and strong points. The plan will take advantage of the strong points, provide corrective solutions for eliminating weaknesses, and suggest entirely new endeavors to be pursued with the subsidiary. The conceptual plan will consist of selection of those factors that are most relevant to positive future results and minimizing those that have negative impact. If negative factors exist, such as a low margin backlog, obsolete products, poor locations, current losses, or other adverse items of this type, the seller should have in the business plan their solutions and if no solutions exist, realize the price resulting from return on investment calculations will automatically be affected. The plan can and should contain such valid concepts as the effects of consolidations, elimination of unprofitable lines or locations, proceeds from liquidations, introduction of new technology, introduction of improved or new marketing, deductions for the effects of non-recurring events, personnel changes, relocations, and the obvious benefit of new management designed to appeal to the ego of any prospective buyer.

Once the concepts are established, the plan should be developed in complete detail with supporting financial projections for both profits and cash flow in order to prove its validity and find the weak portions. The projection must show that under the assumptions of the plan, a buyer would receive a return on investment ample to justify the seller's price. Most buyers will be as concerned over liquidity and projected cash flow as they will be over profit projections, and this important aspect of the plan and forecast cannot be neglected. Projections which show negative cash flow for three or more years or no profits before the third year are also showing the subsidiary is probably unsaleable as a going business. If the seller's projections reveal any of the assumptions to be worthless or of little value, the assumptions should not be used because prospects will eventually come to the same conclusion and use the results to belittle the price.

The price should be such that with a general explanation of the conceptual business plan, but without the aid of elaborate detailed forecasts, a potential buyer will believe a favorable rate of return on investment may be possible for the price and the subsidiary is worth investigating. A prospectve buyer will not believe detailed financial forecasts prepared for prospects by the seller and the seller should not voluntarily give them to the prospect, but the overall conceptual future business plan should be presented as early as possible. Routine internal forecasts and budgets will eventually have to be given the prospect, but these must be represented as internal reports of the subsidiary and not representations of the seller or a business plan for a new owner unless they strongly support the seller's position. Internal subsidiary budgets and forecasts that have a history of reliability and will be vigorously and intelligently defended by the subsidiary management can be very impressive to prospects, but these conditions seldom exist. Let the prospect develop his own forecast based upon his modifications of the conceptual business plan and what appears to be an obvious opportunity for him and conclude for himself the price is reasonable. If the seller's price cannot be easily justified on a return on investment basis, then the price is too high; and it is a waste of time to put forth such a price and seek the ever elusive rich fool. Even if located, his lawyers, accountants, vociferous business school graduates and other advisors will discourage him from proceeding.

A price range within which to set the specific price can be calculated by using comparative investment guidelines. The high point of the range will be the price that has a projected return of one and one-half times that of conservative investments during the second year of ownership. The low point of the range is the price that has a return of three times that of conservative investments during the second year of ownership. A further check on the price to be set within the range is the buyer should receive a total return within five years equal to the total investment. A price at the high end of the range can only be justified for a profitable subsidiary free of major problems, which has excellent growth potential. A price at the low end would be appropriate for a subsidiary presently in a loss position that is beset by major but soluable problems.

Price Parameters

In setting a price the ultimate controlling factor is what a willing buyer can justify after comparing the price with readily available alternate investment opportunities and finding purchase of the subsidiary will produce a superior return. Using this comparative investment method, a price range can be set. The buyer's minimum anticipated annual return for the second year after purchase must be at a level at least 50% greater than the return on relatively risk-free investments such as high grade corporate bonds. The 50% above risk-free investments is an absolute minimum, but it sets the upper limit of the price range. At the lower end of the range, the sellers price need not be so low that a buyer in the second year will have a rate of return greater than three times that of conservative investments.

A buyer will consider the price to be the total investment including essential capital expenditures, new working capital requirements, any losses projected prior to the time the subsidiary becomes profitable less any cash realized by the buyer from immediate asset liquidations. The buyer's total investment should have a return falling between one and one-half and three times that of relatively risk-free investments in the second year of ownership. In any case the buyer should be able to see that if all goes well, the total investment will be recovered within five years. Projected earnings also must be high enough that a buyer's earnings from other operations will not be diluted after the first year of ownership. The following simplified example illustrates the method of calculating the price range.

Assumptions—
1. Prime industrial bonds yield 9%.
2. After-tax earnings are forecast as follows:

1st year	$ (100,000)	loss
2nd year	200,000	profit
3rd year	250,000	profit
4th year	300,000	profit
5th year	350,000	profit
Total	$ 1,000,000	profit

To calculate *low point* of price range—

$$(9\% \times 3) \text{ of price} = \text{2nd year forecast}$$
$$.27 \times \text{price} = \$200,000$$
$$\text{price} = \$740,740$$

To calculate *high point* of price range—

$$(9\% \times 1\frac{1}{2}) \text{ of price} = \text{2nd year forecast}$$
$$13.5 \times \text{price} = \$ 200,000$$
$$\text{price} = \$1,481,481$$

The price range is $740,740 to $1,481,481 with total 5-year earnings of $1,000,000 falling within the range.

Setting the Price

The seller should set the exact price within the range by objectively evaluating the overall quality of the subsidiary with emphasis on probability of the earnings forecast and a buyers maximum potential loss if all goes wrong. Although reflected in return on investment calculations, many factors must be given extra weight. Debt, new borrowing requirements, or capital additions will cause the price to be lower in the range; previously expensed R&D will raise the price in the range; a weak management will depress the price but the opposite condition will cause a higher price. These internal items affect price, but external factors also exist, such as PE ratios of stocks of public companies in the same industry as the subsidiary, the price in recent sales of comparable businesses, and the overall mood and attitude of investors toward the economy as a whole. Should large start-up costs be involved in starting a comparable business, the price can be favorably affected. To further complicate matters, the participants in the process will have independent ideas as to the weight and importance of the various factors. As a result of the internal and external factors, setting a price becomes a subjective exercise regardless of how it is cloaked with mathematics and arguments of the seller. The range and framework established and supported by the conceptual business plan will only provide rational parameters for setting the price.

A need for R&D, capital expenditures, or other capital requirements to achieve a reasonable level of profit must be reflected in pricing. Large amounts of debt, liabilities, financial exposure of unknown amounts, and dubious jobs in progress will adversely affect the price, and prospects will consider these items as part of the total price they must pay. Prospects will be looking at their total investment to make the subsidiary produce the desired return and not just at what they will pay the seller. The rationale for the price will also be necessary for seller internal approvals. No seller will want to sell at a price less than book value, but return on investment calculations can demonstrate it to be a necessity. The calculations may also show a much higher price is justified than anyone realized.

Regardless of the logic of the price established, there always will be those who believe the price is either too high or low or those who lose sight of the primary objective and object to some trivial aspect of the transaction. Whoever makes the final decision on price should just assume the price will never be agreeable with everyone, and expect to be openly or covertly second-guessed by others within the organization. As usual, those with the least experience and facts will be the most willing to criticize. Regardless of what comments are received, someone must make a final decision on price. The seller's ideal price is the maximum the buyer will accept and chances are the seller will never know this number because most buyers won't know either since opinions and positions change during negotiations.

The maximum price developed on a return on investment basis and supported by a conceptual business plan will be an optimum price that the seller can expect to receive. The seller must weigh it against the price required to make divestiture worthwhile when compared with other alternatives. If the reason for sale is the seller's desperate financial condition, the objective is to cut losses or raise funds quickly, then a quick sale will take precedence over considerations of what the subsidiary may fairly be worth. If the seller is not pressed and considers the price resulting from the business plan forecast is too low, then the seller must proceed with other alternatives or reevaluate the minimum price objective. The maximum price within the range may have a sobering effect by showing the objective to be unrealistic, or it may only cause the seller to attempt to develop another conceptual business plan to support a higher price. If a logical and probable business plan cannot be conceived that will support the seller's price expectations and there is no alternative but to sell the subsidiary, then the seller must face up to accepting a lower price.

Assuming the plan supports a price above the seller's minimum acceptable level, the seller should not be deluded into reducing the price in hopes of creating a more attractive price to accelerate the sale. Price reductions will probably have little effect in speeding up the sale unless they are so great they create an extreme, nearly irresistable bargain that only would be justified if the seller was threatened with or was in bankruptcy. An exceptionally low price when the seller is not under pressure to sell could be counterproductive by causing prospects to suspect the subsidiary had concealed or understated problems. If the subsidiary fits with a prospect's general overall program and the price is reasonable, a sale will probably result in about the same time that it would have if the price was modestly reduced. It may eventually be necessary to reduce it in final negotiations but it is inadvisable to do so prematurely.

Decide Upon Terms

Upon setting a price, decisions need to be made regarding acceptable terms. The basic price for the subsidiary is first established on a cash basis in a currency specified by the seller because cash has a specific, known, uniform value that can be quickly understood and used as a basis for term calculations. Very early in any discussions with prospects, the subject of terms will likely surface, and it is best to be in a position to give a clear-cut answer. A practical approach to terms is the strategy of stating a fixed all-cash price but indicating to the buyer that if terms and consideration other than cash are used, then the price will go up. At a later date, accepting terms and agreeing not to raise the price can be treated as a significant concession. Regardless of bargaining strategy, the seller is justified in demanding a higher price for a non-cash transaction but probably will not get it.

The seller must establish the degree of flexibility with regard to terms. If the seller's objective is to raise cash through the sale of a subsidiary, then an all cash price must be insisted upon to meet the sale objective. Even a seller whose objective is all cash should realize it is unlikely receipt of the full purchase price at time of closing will occur. One hundred percent cash at time of closing is enviable but difficult to achieve when the price is a function of the net worth of the company or some other basis that cannot be established until after closing. The buyer may also insist a portion of the price be placed in escrow until the various warranties and representations of the seller are confirmed.

Should the seller be willing to accept less than 100% cash at time of closing and the balance in notes, then there are several important factors to keep in mind in establishing the mimimum down payment. One relates to taxes. If less than 30% of the total consideration is received in cash in a seller's taxable year, it will be treated as an installment sale. In an installment sale, taxes need only be paid on the cash received within the tax year. If the cash received exceeds 30%, then the entire transaction is taxable in the first year. Of course, if the subsidiary is being sold for no profit or at a loss, taxes will not be due under any method of payment. The importance of professional tax advice throughout the sales program cannot be underestimated.

Another factor in determining minimum cash acceptable is that there must be enough cash involved to make it difficult for the buyer to simply walk away at a later date if things do not go well. The greater amount of cash changing hands at closing, the greater the commitment of the buyer. Interest rates on notes accepted must be adequate to avoid imputed interest charges. Generous interest rates may be attractive to the buyer, but they could result in the seller losing a portion of his principal through imputed interest charges. Interest charges of at least the prime rate will prevent this problem. The transaction also must have enough substance to be recorded as a sale under accounting rules. A sale largely for notes that have dubious value because of the quality of the buyer or value of the collateral may only be treated as a sale for reporting purposes as the notes are actually paid off.

When a portion of the consideration is paid in promissory notes, the matter of security for the notes becomes of prime importance. The buyer should be willing to give as security the assets and business purchased, but will reluctantly go beyond that point and give additional collateral, such as guarantees of the buyer's company or personal guarantees. An important part of any negotiations involving promissory notes will center around the security involved with the seller negotiating for as much security as possible and the prudent buyer attempting to reduce the security to a minimum.

Use of Stock

Many potential buyers will prefer to buy with either common or preferred stock. The seller's desire for immediate cash and the quality of the securities will be prime factors in the seller's decision on acceptance of stock. Stock of quality that is readily marketable should be attractive to any seller as well as advantageous to the buyer. A seller should be able to receive a better price, possibly the full asking price, if stock is accepted. When the seller is anxious to dispose of a problem subsidiary and immediate cash is not a prime concern, it may be advantageous to accept securities of the same quality as the subsidiary being sold. In any transaction involving stock the seller will do well to investigate the quality and marketability of the securities regardless of his determination to be rid of the subsidiary.

Contingency Payments

Terms involving contingency payments from the buyer, if certain profit levels are attained or specific orders are received, have both advantages and disadvantages for the parties. Under such provisions an additional amount is paid if certain agreed objectives are achieved. For the seller, the contingency portion of the price will not be bookable until received, because there is no certainty that it will be received. Contingency plans do afford the seller a chance to receive funds he would not have had otherwise. A buyer has the advantage of not paying the higher price unless the subsidiary is a proven profitable performer and he pays at a time when it is affordable. The buyer has the disadvantage of the seller's reviewing and having access to his financial statements, which is a nuisance.

Contingency payments are a means of compromise when the parties are unable to agree upon price; but, unless carefully constructed with complete and precise guidelines, these agreements can cause more disputes than their worth and easily precipitate legal action. The guidelines must include a definition of income that will be applicable regardless of any changes made in the subsidiary by the buyer. A contingency payment plan is not as desirable as cash plus secured notes, but in some situations it may be the only way to reach agreement. A subsidiary with a poor earnings history but with excellent future prospects may lend itself to this type of transaction. The buyer will be saying, "If this business is as good as you (the seller) claim, then you eventually will receive your price." The seller's counter argument is, "It will be as good as we say if properly managed, but we will not be responsible for your management."

Merchandise Credits

In some transactions, a merchandise credit may be a possibility. A merchandise credit is a device for discounting the price to the buyer and also a means of holding out the hope that a business relationship will exist beyond the life of the merchandise credit. If the subsidiary sold has been a supplier to other parts of the seller's corporation, then a merchandise credit arrangement is relatively easy and attractive to structure. Should the buyer be a producer of other goods or services that are purchased by the seller, a merchandise credit arrangement is possible. There are problems associated with merchandise credits. If the merchandise credit is not used within a year, imputed interest charges may be incurred by the buyer. The buyer in a merchandise credit agreement will have a peculiar tax obligation in that the profit on the merchandise transferred to the seller will be treated as taxable income although no cash has actually changed hands. Again, this is a situation that will require professional tax assistance.

Other Pricing Considerations

To sell the subsidiary at all, the seller may find it necessary to retain an equity position in the subsidiary and thus reduce the price. A buyer may find this attractive in that the seller is still tied in with whatever he has represented the subsidiary to be. The seller will also have an obligation to provide some input into the subsidiary to protect his interests. Regardless of whether the buyer intends to eventually purchase the remainder of the seller's interest or the parties expect to continue the relationship forever, a contractual agreement should be agreed upon at the onset that provides a right of first refusal for one party to buy out the other's interest on the basis of a predetermined formula. It is far easier to agree upon the formula when everyone is in a cooperative frame of mind and are discussing what may or may not be the conditions in the future rather than at a time when the situation may have changed drastically from what one or both parties anticipated. If a seller elects to sell only a portion of his interest and sells it for less than book value, he will have to write down the shares retained to the value of those sold. If a seller retained a substantial portion of shares under such conditions, he could receive an unwelcome and unexpected shock.

Because of the different requirements of sellers and the ability of buyers and the endless opportunity to conceive and negotiate over terms, an infinite number of combinations of cash, stock, notes, debentures, contingency payments, and merchandise credits may result in a satisfactory agreement for the parties. There are no guidelines that are universally applicable to all transactions, except that a flexible approach will most often accommodate the needs of both parties and bring about agreement. Each side should work to perceive and assist in solving the other's problems but try to keep the solutions simple.

Before finalizing the price, the seller should review the price from the viewpoint of potential buyers and look at their downside risk or maximum loss possible if everything goes wrong. Prospective buyers will correctly or incorrectly assume there is plenty wrong with the subsidiary or it would not be for sale. Some devil's advocate in the buyer's organization will be asking, "What happens if it doesn't work out?" Substantial assets that may be liquidated will be reassuring to the buyer. The seller should be aware of the buyer's downside risk and, in his presentation, stress the lack of risk if such is the case and keep quiet if it is not.

A final consideration in establishing a price is the question of what additional inducements can be offered to a buyer, such as future business with the subsidiary sold or business with other parts of the corporation. By offering to the prospective buyer the opportunity to work closely with the seller in other areas, the seller may provide the critical factor in making the price acceptable. Purchase of the subsidiary becomes the overall price of admission. This approach is most practical when the seller is a large corporation and the buyer also is a sizeable corporation with its subsidiaries either customers or suppliers of the seller. The prospect of joint ventures in the international area may also be a further inducement to make the price acceptable. When inducements of this type are possible, the seller should be careful not to make promises that cannot or will not be kept. The seller should also avoid promises that will be delegated to subsidiaries or others for follow-up activities. People do not always perform as expected regardless of who is the boss.

With the structure of the transaction determined, a reasonable price established, and bargaining latitude on terms developed, a final review of the seller's alternatives other than divestment is still in order. The full process of organizing to sell can commence upon completion of that review and the final decision to sell is made.

6.
Organizing
to Sell

Utilizing Personnel

The corporation wishing to divest a subsidiary must assess its personnel, weigh them against the requirements of a sales program, and then decide who will participate and what will be their respective roles. It is unlikely that experienced and competent personnel will be readily available just standing by to fully staff the ideal organization because few companies are of sufficient size and have continuous divestiture requirements that would justify a permanent staff. However, whenever possible, members for the selling organization should be selected with the idea in mind that they may be needed again and will become permanent corporate specialists in divestiture.

Depending upon the importance of the divestment to the seller and the availability of employees, personnel will either be temporarily borrowed from other positions within the seller's organization or outside professionals brought in to staff and implement the program. A sales program, whether voluntary or, as in the case of a bankruptcy, involuntary, consists of certain essential elements to be accomplished if success is to be achieved. A seller should first consider the basic elements of what is to be accomplished and then make personnel assignments so that all aspects are properly covered. In assigning responsibilities and planning the program in a large corporation, the roles group, division or regional executives, and employees will play must be considered, because these levels of management between parent and subsidiary cannot be ignored. This will vary within each corporation depending upon the organizational structure and ability of individuals involved. The eight following key elements, all of which require personnel and time, should be recognized, evaluated, and

74

properly assigned with everyone involved being informed of their responsibilities and assignments:

1. Major decision making
2. Overall management and planning
3. Day-to-day supervision
4. Data gathering
5. Contact and selling of prospects
6. Negotiating
7. Documentation and closing
8. Transition

Major Decision Making

This includes such decisions as whether or not the subsidiary is to be sold at all, the timing for the commencement of the sales program, the price, terms, who is responsible, and the final approval or disapproval of whatever agreement is tentatively reached with a prospective buyer. These decisions will normally be made by the board of directors; but in companies with a strong chief executive and an obliging board the chief executive may make the major decisions. In some cases the final authority may be a judge or bankruptcy referee. Whatever the power structure may be, divestments will require some involvement of whoever or whatever individual or group has ultimate and final authority.

Overall Management and Planning

The quality of the overall management and planning of the entire program, as in most endeavors or institutions, will largely determine its success. The management, planning, implementation, and motivation of those involved requires senior management experience, and a person of this caliber should be assigned full responsibility for the success of the program. This person's role will include deciding upon what information is needed and seeing that it is secured on a timely basis, presentation of recommendations to whoever is responsible for major decisions, selection of those to participate in the program, and overseeing the selling team activities to ensure maximum performance. Planning the sales presentations, deciding upon which prospects to contact, and supervising the negotiations will also be areas of responsibility along with the eventual closing activities.

Day-to-Day Supervision

Day-to-day supervision in sales programs makes certain that the program runs on schedule and the seller is always in the position of waiting for the buyer's next move rather than the buyer's decision-making process being delayed by failure of the seller to provide requested data or arrange requested meetings. This activity also involves scheduling of contacts with prospects and planning of follow-up contacts as circumstances warrant. Constant supervision aids in meeting time schedules and keeping the sales team working at an optimum pace.

Data Gathering

Data gathering begins before the decision to sell is made and continues through the negotiations and closing. While much of the data is financial, a broad range of other data about the business as enumerated in Appendixes A and B is also required. In these programs, there seldom will be enough data and new requirements will continually emerge. Data gathering will eventually end with the investigations to support negotiations concerning the seller's representations and warranties and with the preparation of whatever exhibits are required as attachments to the definitive final contract.

Contact and Selling of Prospects

Contact and selling of prospects must occur prior to negotiations. Prospects need be informed of the subsidiary for sale in a manner that will induce them to investigate further and eventually buy. This is the process of notifying prospects of the possibility, creating interest, presenting reasons why they should buy, and arranging for their inspection of the business. It also would include the development and distribution of promotional literature and whatever entertainment of prospects is necessary.

Negotiating

Negotiating involves the give and take arguments in which both parties strive to maximize or preserve their respective positions. It includes the formal negotiations with the parties sitting on opposite sides of a table and the informal where principals meet in private or in small groups to resolve basic or stubborn issues. Negotiations also include the preparations prior to sessions and the frequent discussions or supplemental negotiations once a letter of intent is signed or a preliminary agreement is reached. Sales of complete businesses are complex transactions in which only a general accord covering major items such as price and terms is first achieved, but many other minor decisions and agreements must be settled as they emerge for inclusion in a definitive agreement. Negotiations often continue right up until the final contract is signed.

Documentation and Closing

Documentation of transactions into formal contracts and the signing at closing represents the conclusion of a divestiture program. This documentation is voluminous and takes attorneys and accountants weeks to prepare. Participants are appalled and offended by the length of the contracts and exhibits but few are able to suggest any items for deletion. The final act of documentation is the recording of the transaction in the seller's financial records and statements.

Transition

Transition activities usually start before the actual closing occurs. The buyer will often want access to the facility and employees so that upon the day of closing the sale control can immediately be taken without delays for learning. Since almost all divested subsidiaries have problems of varying magnitude, the buyer will want to be in a position to take quick action once control has been assumed. After closing there usually remain continuing or unsettled matters that involve the seller. Someone must be appointed to look after the seller's interests and be a point of contact for the buyer. Transitional activities can range from the negligible, such as providing miscellaneous information, to major tasks, such as administration of a merchandise credit or collection of receivables excluded from the transaction. The representative of the seller responsible for transitional activity can play a key role prior to closing by providing full cooperation and assistance to the buyer and thus help maintain the buyer's enthusiasm for the deal.

Combining Responsibility

All of the essential elements could conceivably be handled by one person but such is not practical or warranted in transactions of any magnitude. The total number of people involved will be a function of personnel availability, their abilities, the organization and internal political structure of the seller, and the importance of the transaction to the seller. Usually, a large staff is not required and one to three people exclusive of accountants and attorneys will be sufficient. Generally, one individual will handle several functions, such as the overall management and planning of the sales program and also conduct the day-to-day supervision. Data may be accumulated by people who will also be involved in making the actual contact or sales calls. Those making the sales contacts may very well participate in or conduct the negotiations, because it would provide continuity and capitalize on any rapport developed during their contact with the prospect.

Equally possible is for several people to be involved in only one of the elements. For example, a number of people may be out contacting prospects or participate in data gathering. Data gathering consists of gathering the initial data, updating the data during the program, and handling special requests for supplemental data for prospects. Ideally, this activity would all be the responsibility of one individual or a team headed by one individual; but it could be accomplished by several different individuals as the program progressed. Obviously, how well any of these elements is handled depends upon the overall competence and ability of the individuals assigned.

Another example indicating how several individuals could be involved is in the area of decision making. Essentially, there are major decisions and minor decisions to be made throughout the program. Major decisions include whether or not one will sell at all and the general pricing parameters. Minor decisions consisting of what prospects should be contacted next and the timing of such contacts could very well be made by someone else on a day-to-day basis. The key elements in the program must be provided for with proper assignments because the program will fail if any are omitted. There is too much at stake in a divestment to not provide the means of accomplishing the program.

Program Management

Divestment will probably involve the chief executive officer of the corporation. The chief executive officer must create the overall organization and sales program, secure whatever board approvals are necessary, be available to make decisions, be an enthusiastic unwavering backer of the program, and keep motivated the direct participants in the program during the various ups and downs that normally occur. The chief executive should also be available to meet with the chief executive of another corporation believed to be a likely prospect. First contacts by the chief executive officer should be limited to a few select situations where either he is personally acquainted with the chief executive of the prospect, or there is reason to believe a high probability exists the prospect will have a strong interest in exploring acquisition of the subsidiary. He will become a sorry spectacle if he engages in a large number of direct contacts.

The chief executive should disengage his ego and engage in a certain amount of introspection and privately assess his own strengths and weaknesses as to what can be contributed by direct participation with prospects. Unless the chief executive officer is a superb salesman and negotiator, who has a total grasp of all the details surrounding the operations of the subsidiary to be sold, it would be best for him not to participate directly with prospects. Participation when ill prepared could easily lead to unfortunate decisions, and, when the chief executive makes the decisions in a negotiation, there is little opportunity to back off or refer the decision to higher authority. A divestiture program requires strong management control, time, and leadership and if the chief executive does not fill this role because of other demands on his time or the relative unimportance of a small divestiture, then some other executive must fill this role. In very large corporations, a portion of the role of a chief executive officer in a divestiture may be assigned to a group or divisional executive if the divestiture is not large.

Ideally, a key senior executive, reporting directly to the chief executive officer, should be assigned responsibility for planning, management and day-to-day activities of the program including sales contact and negotiations with the senior personnel of prospects. This individual must have the status to give him the necessary credibility to be effective in negotiations and, as much as possible, be something of an all-around person. Such an individual should have sales ability and have enough business experience to fully understand accounting and conduct detailed negotiations that are associated with the sale of a business. This person must have ready access to the chief executive officer to secure timely decisions, and time to devote to the program. This program will be part-time for six to eight weeks at the start in order to plan, organize, and gather data, and nearly full-time for another five to six weeks once negotiations with a prospect commence.

The complexity and amount of time necessary to conduct a program of any magnitude should never be underestimated thus compounding the difficulty in finding the competent senior executive who can be released from other assignments. A possible candidate for this senior position would be the executive responsible for the acquisition program because such an individual would have knowledge of negotiating and knowledge of what is involved in the sale of a business, but only larger firms have such people. Others possible may be a senior executive who is about to retire or can be called back from retirement or an executive between major positions or about to be promoted. A promising middle management executive who exhibits exceptional judgment may be given the assignment as a challenge and broadening experience. If it can be avoided, the executive with direct operating responsibility for the divestment should not be assigned the job of selling the subsidiary. Too many conflicts of interest between operations and selling develop that will impede the success of the program.

Accounting and Legal
Services

A senior accountant should be assigned to the program to oversee data gathering and be available throughout the entire program. This person will be responsible for accumulating and developing all data required for the evaluation, decision making, and presentation to the prospect. As the program progresses, the senior accountant should be responsible for receiving updates on the financial condition of the company and communicating such to those involved in the sales effort. He should be available to supply data for special requests for information not previously prepared but now requested by a prospect. The accountant ideally is a permanent employee that can remain with the program throughout its duration. This individual should have a reasonable amount of personality and sales ability as well as a strong loyalty to the seller. Responsibilities will include working with the auditors of prospective buyers and other financial people sent in to evaluate the subsidiary. He should be able to readily provide information to prospects and gain their confidence by having a complete grasp of all financial data associated with the subsidiary. He also must have the good judgment as to what should not be provided to prospects and how to avoid volunteering data not helpful to the sale. In some sales, the buyers are so determined they do not want to learn of bad news. The accountant can be helpful in establishing supplemental lines of communication through the accountants of the prospect during the bargaining period. Subtle and not so subtle communication through this avenue can be very helpful in bringing the parties together in negotiations by enlightening each other as to their problems without principals having to make such statements or admit to a set of facts. If a senior internal accountant cannot be assigned to the program, it is possible to have a public accountant or consulting firm supply one with the consultant approach preferable to avoid ethical or conflict of interest problems.

Legal assistance will inevitably become required once a preliminary agreement is reached, but legal advice is valuable before this time. The earlier an attorney is brought into the program the better, because no attorney can draft a contract covering a transaction he does not understand. An attorney can advise on how to structure the sale, investigate legal problems, and if appropriate, participate directly in the negotiations. How soon an attorney is brought into the negotiations depends upon the specific facts of the situation. A seller with competent in-house lawyers may wish to use them as principal negotiators.

Subsidiary Employee Involvement

Personnel of the subsidiary to be divested will eventually be involved, if only in the minor way of being interviewed or acting as guides. The seller must be extremely cautious because of the employee's awkward position and ambivalent loyalties during such a period. Regardless of the sentiments or attitudes professed by the subsidiary's employees, the seller has no way to hide the employees because they are important assets the prospect, it is hoped, will buy. Employees may be bitter, indifferent, or enthusiastic about the prospect of the sale, but nearly all will have strong views as to how the subsidiary could have been operated more effectively and profitably. Consequently, many are overly optimistic about the potential of the subsidiary which will help the seller. Their attitudes often are mixed, and the seller should not be overconfident in predicting how they will perform when they meet with the prospective buyers. They may be antagonistic, overly candid, and totally unrealistic; but a buyer will not disregard their views without full evaluation. The closer one moves towards an actual sale being consummated with a prospect, the more open with a prospect they will become and the less open with the seller. Sometime prior to an actual closing, the loyalties of the employees will begin to transfer to the prospective buyer; and the seller should never forget this fact. The seller may as well disclose all important facts about the subsidiary and not be deluded in thinking that the employees will keep anything secret. Before closing and when closing seems a certainty, they for all practical purposes will be the employees of the buyer.

Sales personnel of the subsidiary may be enlisted to contact less probable prospects, but these should be limited to initial contacts and their activities carefully structured. They should be trained to present the material which they have been asked to present and, if there is a spark of interest, arrange for the prospects to meet with senior officials of the selling company.

The Chief Negotiator

In the planning of the selling organization, thought should be given to the negotiating process and the individual who will be the seller's chief negotiator. Negotiations with prospects could occur within days after the commencement of the contact with prospects so this aspect of the program must be well thought out in advance. The seller's negotiator should be a person with proven successful experience in this type of negotiation and a person of stature that the prospects will respect and believe. Negotiations have less chance of being productive if a buyer's chief negotiator finds a counterpart to be inexperienced, of low ability, and possessing less status. The seller's negotiator can be superior in ability and stature without damaging the negotiations, but not inferior. Regardless of the ability and track record of the chief negotiator, the seller should not expect miracles. A top negotiator will be quick to define what is probable and what is unlikely to occur and what is the likely result of a negotiation.

If no suitable executives of the seller are qualified or available as chief negotiator, then an experienced attorney or consultant should be selected. There is too much at stake in a divestiture negotiation for a seller to use an inexperienced negotiator. Attorneys or consultants as professionals seem to have a universal status that makes it possible for them to deal with executives of any level, providing they have obvious competence and ability. Whoever is selected for this role should be introduced as early as possible to the prospects in order to have time to build some rapport. The so-called master negotiator, who can step into negotiations at the last minute without preparation or having a chance to develop rapport and then quickly negotiate brilliant contracts bringing about a counterpart's capitulation, just does not exist. Quick negotiations more than likely involve the seller's capitulation. Complete preparation plus experience in negotiations will be more productive than super negotiating skills and techniques. The super salesman-negotiator type approach may have some application for sales of vacuum cleaners or brushes but not for divestitures where the prospects are sophisticated and it is several months after negotiations before closing occurs allowing ample time for a "victim" to reconsider.

A negotiating team has some advantages but it also has major disadvantages. A team brings a broader range of specialties to the bargaining table, but someone still must be the chief spokesman. A perceptive buyer will be quick to perceive who is the senior member of the negotiating team and look only to him for key decisions and moves. Multiple spokesmen eventually find themselves in conflict with each other to the delight of their counterparts. A seller will be wise to have it firmly understood that there will only be one spokesman and chief negotiator regardless of the size of the negotiating team.

In organizing the program, the chief negotiator must be not only given bargaining latitude, but must also have a structure within which to work where he can quickly secure new instructions as conditions change. A system for quick decisions will make it unnecessary for the negotiator to exceed his authority in an effort to preserve the negotiations. Reversal of a position a negotiator has taken may mean permanent impairment of the negotiator's credibility with the prospect and thus reduce or totally destroy his ability to continue. The chief negotiator should not be placed in the position where his most difficult problems and negotiations are with the people in his own organization. He needs stature within his organization since he may find his most troublesome negotiations on his own side of the table. A negotiator may find himself playing an informal role of mediator as well as negotiator when members of the seller's management group need to be enlightened as to the realities of the situation.

The chief negotiator should have clear cut guidelines and bargaining latitude with the emphasis on the major objectives rather than on peripheral issues. The major objectives are to sell the subsidiary for a price as close to the asking price as possible for the type consideration agreed to be acceptable. The skilled negotiator will hold fast to the major objectives and be generous in concessions on other matters of lesser importance. The internal second-guessers will concentrate on the minor items much to the annoyance of the negotiators. Second guessing by those far from the realities of the bargaining table will always exist, but a wise president will do well to discourage this type of debilitating activity.

Use of Outsiders

The corporation will have to assess the importance of the divestment to the total corporation against the availability of personnel and evaluate the effect of diverting competent personnel from their current activities to work on the divestment program. Ideally, the seller has ample competent employees to implement the program in its entirety but lack of internal manpower may force the use of outsiders. The use of outsiders such as consultants, brokers, and investment bankers or the degree of their utilization will become an area for early and major decisions. In some unfortunate situations where the seller must sell subsidiaries to survive and has no internal staff available, he is in about the same situation and at the same disadvantage as the grieving family calling in the undertaker to pick up the body. Use of nonemployees can range from not at all to a supplement to the internal organization to taking full responsibility for the entire program. However, if the seller has competent, experienced in-house personnel who are willing to plan and learn, there will be little need; and he will be better off not to use the outsiders other than in a very limited way for training or for initial contact of prospects in out-of-the-way locations.

Outside consultants, who have successfully planned and implemented divestments, can be extremely helpful to sellers with limited experience because of their broader exposure and normally systematic approach. However, there are not large numbers of such people available who have proven records, and they must be carefully examined before contracting for their services. Particular care must be taken to make certain the individual consultant who will work on the project will be one who has had extensive experience and demonstrated success. Overall experience by the firm with which a consultant is associated is of little or no value if the consultant assigned is inexperienced. However, strong competent consultants may be more than worth their cost, which is usually charged on a per diem rather than a success basis. Consultants can provide the personnel for the program if such is not available internally. They can be helpful in placing the program on a realistic basis where expectations are neither too high nor too low. An outsider's view as to what can be realistically expected is always of value to management and a competent consultant's dispassionate observations can greatly aid the program.

A number of consulting firms have developed a specialty in helping owners sell their companies and in divestments and a few claim to specialize in divestitures alone. All these people require close scrutiny before becoming involved and direct discussion with prior clients is a necessity. Try to talk to as many clients as possible including those for which they were unsuccessful. Failure may not be a reflection upon the ability of the consultants because the seller may have been the cause of the failure. The investigation before agreeing to their services should include a review of mailings and sales presentations for other clients. Often this material is more an advertisement for the consulting firm than for the client's divestiture. Advertising of this type at a client's expense should not be looked upon favorably.

Investment Banking Firms

Investment banking firms are worth considering when neither internal personnel nor a competent consulting group are available. Great care should be taken in utilizing the investment bankers because most claim competence but a far lesser number possess it. In all cases the seller should demand to know what other divestitures they have handled and what specifically was the role they played and the service provided. Even with those firms with positive reputations the seller should again be cautious in evaluating the experience of the individual assigned to work on the divestment. Many of these firms experience frequent turnover in personnel, and they lose interest in projects that prove to be difficult or long-term because of their desire for a quick, large fee. Regardless of what they initially state, compensation arrangements with investment bankers are usually highly negotiable. Some companies have such a close relationship with an investment banker at their board of directors level that it may prove politically difficult not to utilize their services in some manner.

Business Brokers

Lower on the scale are the independent business brokers who have proliferated throughout the business world. These people are primarily active as finders and normally have little experience in planning a program. Undoubtedly there are exceptions, but they will be difficult to discover. Care should be taken not to enter into any agreement with the independent brokers or with investment banking firms whereby one would agree to allow them to manage or assist in the divestment with an exclusive arrangement. Independent brokers normally work on a success basis.

Conflict of Interest

In using any outside group, whether it is an independent consultant, an investment banker or broker, there always is the possibility of a conflict of interest. All claim to have great integrity and most do, but the potential for conflicts of interest because of their diverse clients and the large sums of money involved create severe temptations. The best safeguard in selecting outsiders is to demand their record of performance in similar situations. A seller should never be content with only the reputation of the firm or the consultant assigned but should contact their prior clients and verify the results.

Full Information Available

Every individual, whether employee or outsider employed for the program who will have contact with prospects, should have as complete a knowledge of the business and industry as possible. This should be extensive information that will permit the representative of the seller to answer all but the most obscure questions and by being able to do so, move along the proceedings and effectively establish credibility. In addition to having a full understanding of the financials, the representative must be conversant in the subsidiary's history, its main business activity, method of distribution, total markets, background of the management and "tip of the tongue" familiarity with all items listed in Appendixes A and B. Knowledge of the overall industry and its problems and maximum data on competitors will be especially helpful. The seller's representative should approach prospects confidently as experts ready for any questions.

Once the seller has decided upon the staff he will employ to effect the divestment, he is ready to start with his overall sales program. It is desirable for all those who are assigned activities and responsibilities of the sales program to become involved in the overall development of the program from the very start. The more involved the better will be the understanding and the greater will be the possibility for a flow of ideas, an imaginative approach, and a comprehensive plan.

7.
Employees
Are Assets

The need for frequent, thoughtful decisions and the effect of those decisions in a divestiture program upon the employees has been commented upon often. Not only does an employer have legal and moral obligations to employees, but the employees represent important assets of the business which, if neglected or mistreated, could vanish or become assets of little value. The employees either directly or indirectly through their actions do have a major influence upon the sale, and this fact should never be forgotten or underestimated. Generally, any business is more valuable with employees and management than it is without. The greater the competence of the employees, and particularly the management, the more valuable is the subsidiary. A sale of the subsidiary as a going business will be more difficult if it does not have an able staff of employees but facilitated if it has a full complement who are enthusiastic and diligent. Even if the buyer has plans to replace or eliminate some of the management or employees, the buyer will need most of the employees for at least a while. Anyone who has had the experience of staffing a totally new operation from scratch would have an understanding of the importance of having an available staff and the difficulties of restaffing.

When a subsidiary to be sold is losing money, there is a tendency to think in terms of shutting it down to avoid or minimize losses. If the losses are not overly severe and the seller has the financial resources to sustain those losses during a period of time adequate to complete a sale, then a shutdown and termination of all employees is to be avoided. Without employees, the buyer can only expect to receive, at best, little more than liquidation value for the business. A shutdown will also produce the severence expenses associated with shutdown activity which may be prohibitively large.

87

Employee Stability

Sellers frequently are concerned the employees of the subsidiary will quit during the period of the sales program. With reasonable care and providing the sales program does not last indefinitely, such concerns are groundless. Experience shows that employees in an operation about to be sold as a going business normally do not quit. Whatever their motivation, they stay put. They may simply have no other jobs to go to or they may be somewhat disenchanted with the current owners and feel any change will be an improvement. They may recognize the situation as a personal opportunity and believe the new owner will more fully appreciate their talents and labors. They may believe a new owner must have them and will be receptive if they drive a hard bargain. However, they should be cautioned to avoid this approach since gains achieved by such coercion could prove to be temporary. Once the new owner had control and developed his alternatives, the employees who drove the hard bargain could soon find they had little bargaining power left.

Most employees of any business feel that it could be run better. Conditions change and there is always room for improvement in the best of run companies, and they will assume a new owner will make desirable changes. They may believe that the existing management will be improved or possibly that the parent company has never unstood the subsidiary and failed to appreciate its potential. The fact that the subsidiary is now for sale indicates there will be changes, and the employees should be persuaded the odds favor changes for the better.

If the divestment decision was made as a result of poor performance of the subsidiary, the parent management may feel let down and have little sympathy or concern for the employees. Such feelings, whether justified or not, should be concealed, because their surfacing can contribute nothing towards furthering the sale. With the decision to sell the subsidiary, the seller's best interests lie in enlisting the aid of the employees in the sale. A speedy sale is a quick, painless way to part company with the unwanted employees. If the selling parent company's management has little regard for the management and employees of the subsidiary about to be sold, then they can reasonably assume the employees of that subsidiary feel the same towards them. There is no better way for this relationship to end than for the entire group to be sold.

Informing Employees of the Sale

The best policy with the employees is to inform them the subsidiary is for sale shortly after the decision is made and give the reasons. It may become necessary to inform the employees before the final decision is made that such is being contemplated, particularly in cases where substantial investigative work is required or when bargaining with a union is involved. Explain that the new owner will need them, and it is in their best interest to remain and do their finest work during the sales period. Caution them that it will be a time of rumors, strange visitors will be appearing, and that the sale of the subsidiary is a complicated, time-consuming transaction that will not happen overnight. They should be warned that five months will be the minimum length of time necessary to consummate a sale, and probably it will be much longer.

During the selling period, they should from time to time be given some indication of the progress of the sale; and they should be encouraged to ask questions and report rumors as they develop. Occasionally, rumors of prospect activity have enough factual content to be valuable to the personnel responsible for the sale. It is impossible to keep a prolonged program secret, and there is no need to do so. Make the employees a part of the overall program and enlist their aid.

The employees will want to know how the sale will affect the various benefit programs, in particular pensions, vacation rights, special compensation plans such as stock purchases, commissions or bonuses, their length of service, termination pay, etc. The seller should have answers to all of these questions preferably before notifying the employees that a sale is definitely being considered or that the sales program is underway. The seller can be certain these questions will come up and will come up repeatedly until satisfactory answers are given.

Special termination pay or bonus arrangements may be in order in certain cases if extreme conditions exist that would cause it to be difficult to retain employees. Conditions would have to be very extreme to warrant such payments, and a seller should slowly assess the problem before volunteering these payments. Such bonuses, if paid, could best be paid after the employees have spent a minimum period of time with the new owner.

Eventually the buyer will want to meet the employees, and these meetings may have a strong influence on the prospective buyer. If the employees make a favorable impression, the sale will be moved along. Conversely, if the employees are disgruntled and make a bad impression, the prospect may be discouraged. Employees can be enthusiastic in talking to prospective buyers and quite helpful. They should be advised to answer all questions fully and freely. As tactfully as possible, they should be advised not to volunteer large amounts of unnecessary information or bad news that can be presented better by other means. The seller must not appear to have "gagged" employees or censored their comments. Worst of all, the seller should not become involved in instructing the employees to cover up or falsify data, if for no other reason than the high probability of being discovered. A seller simply should not attempt to enlist the aid of employees in a scheme that is devious or less than honorable.

Unsolicited Employee "Assistance"

Often during a sales program, management and other aggressive employees of the subsidiary will take it upon themselves to locate prospects or to make unauthorized contacts with prospects because they believe they could best present the story of the virtues of the company. Unsolicited assistance is seldom damaging to the overall efforts of the seller, but it does become highly frustrating and irritating to those responsible for the sale. Assistance of this type may conflict with overall strategy or result in presentations contradictory to those already presented. Inconsistent statements can occur in these situations easily enough because of the conflicting viewpoints.

All in all, it is best to take the chances that nothing will go wrong as a result of unsolicited assistance on the part of subsidiary personnel rather than establish a prohibitive policy stating that under no condition should they make any unauthorized contacts. To do so would run the greater risk of their concealing the very prospect who may be the most logical buyer. The seller should enlist their aid and request them to bring to the selling group's attention all possible prospects but ask them to advise of any contemplated contacts. This approach can be presented in such a way that they will not be discouraged but will enthusiastically support the program.

8.
Developing
a Sales Program

After selection of the required staff and assignment of their responsibilities, preparation of the detailed sales program may commence. The rationale for selling and for buying must be thoroughly developed and committed to writing. Time schedules for action must be finalized. Complete sales presentations must be prepared, reviewed, and rehearsed. Activity, coordination, and dissemination of information and decisions should begin on an established schedule. A combination of why a subsidiary is for sale and why a prospect should buy will constitute the basic sales presentation.

Establishing a Rationale

The first step in the development of a sound sales program is the finalization of the rationale for selling the subsidiary and why someone would find it advantageous to purchase the subsidiary. This provides the overall philosophical base necessary for an effective program and from which all activity can logically flow. Without this base, the program will be disorganized, inconsistent, unconvincing, and have a low probability of success.

Why it is for sale is important, but the emphasis should be on why anyone should buy because those reasons will ultimately determine the success of the program. The reasons for buying must first convince those involved and representing the seller in the sales program that the subsidiary for the price asked represents a fine business opportunity for the right buyer. If the seller's representatives are not convinced, they will have great difficulty with prospects when they must be enthusiastic advocates.

Once the convincing reasons why someone should buy are fashioned into a total concept, the content of promotional literature and sales presentations will be relatively easy. The identification of possible prospects will be simplified by systematically applying the reasons to buy to categories of prospects to find where they are most applicable. Time will not be wasted on prospects who eventually will discover they actually have no reason to buy. The negotiators will know their best arguments as well as their weak ones. Any sales program should emphasize the valid positive reasons why someone should buy and minimize the negative factors with counterarguments or by pointing out they are outweighed by positive factors. In developing the sales program, a full awareness of all negative factors must exist, and the selling team must perfect in advance its arguments and position on how each negative factor will be treated to reduce its impact when it becomes known to a prospect.

Decide Reasons for Selling

First the seller must decide what are the actual reasons for selling and how will this rationale be publicly presented. One of the early questions any buyer will ask when contact occurs is why is the subsidiary for sale. The seller can present a valid reason or combination of reasons as to why it is for sale as an introduction for why it has not been more successful, regardless of its profitability. This can serve as an avenue to demonstrate to the interested prospect how, under his new and brilliant direction, it can be extremely profitable.

In developing a rationale for the sale, the seller should assume that it is not possible to deceive anyone; and, from the standpoint of concluding a successful sale, only the truth, regardless of its nature, will be effective. Truthful presentation of awkward or embarassing reasons for selling will help establish the seller's integrity with prospects at an early time because most will not expect degrading candor. The seller's executives' rationalization of the subsidiary's problems, particularly those emotionally involved or so distant from the subsidiary that they actually do not fully understand it, must be guarded against and carefully evaluated for accuracy. Managements prefer to conceal their failures although they will argue a certain percentage of mistakes are normal and to be expected. Such logic does not make problem subsidiaries any less painful for those responsible. If the seller finds himself laboring too long on this subject, he should simply ask himself, "Why not tell the truth?" Truthful reasons are not only easy to give, but they are the only ones that will survive the evaluation and negotiation process. All too few sellers seem able to comprehend this fact or are unaware of the determination of buyers in pursuing the subject. Prospects will concentrate on why the subsidiary is for sale until they are totally satisfied that they have the true reasons. Part of their motivation is their belief that this will give further insight into the condition of the subsidiary and possible weaknesses in the bargaining position of the seller.

It is not uncommon for there to be numerous reasons why a subsidiary is for sale; and different executives within the selling company may have varying views as to which reasons are of greatest importance. Perhaps no one reason specifically produced the final decision to sell but a series of events and circumstances. Conflicting reasons for selling, which come to the attention of prospects, will give the impression that far more is wrong with the subsidiary than actually exists and can even cast doubt upon the integrity of the seller. Therefore, one firm reason or a combination of reasons should be developed, written to ensure consistency, and then presented uniformly to all concerned. This should be the official, exclusive rationale known throughout the selling corporation. This official rationale will be used in discussions with prospects, in notification to employees and shareholders, and in formal releases to the media. Its potential distribution is broad and many individuals with diverse interests and backgrounds will be evaluating the official reasons so only a precise and accurate statement will be totally accepted.

There is an endless list of possible reasons, but the great majority of divestitures will be caused by a relatively small number of basic conditions and circumstances that deserve some comment.

New Directions

The seller may wish to divert his resources and energy into other areas and change the total nature of the business. This is certainly a valid reason, and it is the one most commonly given; but it is so common that hardly anyone will accept it regardless of its accuracy. Actually it is valid and accurate in all cases because every divestiture is, to some degree, a realignment of resources, change in allocation of management energy, and shift in business strategy; but it is such an oversimplification that prospects will believe it to be only part of the story. Events had to occur and conditions must exist that caused the basic change and prospects will ferret them out. Grand master plans for reorganizing, redirecting, and restructuring corporations through divestments or acquisitions always make interesting reading, but prospective buyers will be skeptical in inverse proportion to the subsidiary's profitability and will want to know why such changes are thought worthwhile. If the subsidiary's profits are assured for the indefinite future, the new-business rationale will be accepted with less skepticism. The change-of-business rationale, because of its universal applicability, can be effectively used in initial published statements or correspondence with prospects when the seller does not want to fully disclose in writing all of his reasons. This will satisfy the uninvolved and uninitiated, give the sophisticated a laugh, and buy time until face-to-face meetings with prospects occur and a more comprehensive explanation is presented. It also constitutes a bland public statement that will not cause prospects embarrassment. The seller must avoid giving a reason for selling that will make a buyer appear a fool for buying or even showing interest.

Subsidiary Unrelated to Basic Business

The seller may advance the proposition that the subsidiary has not been successful or it has only had limited success because it was not part of an organization that had complementary product lines or activities, thus suggesting the prospective buyer's organization would be an ideal new home. The subsidiary that is totally unrelated either through product line, service lines, or distribution to any other main activities of the selling corporation will seldom receive the full support and knowledgeable direction that a subsidiary requires and, therefore is a reasonable candidate for sale. This can be argued quite successfully because of the logic and obviousness of such a situation when it truly exists. The seller here combines his reason for selling with arguments for buying by saying, "Look, the subsidiary performed at its present level although we were unable to contribute anything substantial to it, but your organization can contribute and you can visualize better than we just how profitable it could become under your control."

The ideal condition prevails when the seller has no great incentive to sell the subsidiary and it would continue to do reasonably well under his control, but it will do much better as part of a company that has related activities. Under these circumstances, a sale could benefit everyone; the seller, the buyer, the subsidiary, and its employees. A buyer should be able to justify paying a higher than normal price and will probably be required to do so.

Incompatible Managements

Often a supplementary reason for sale is that one or two key members of the seller's senior management organization have had personality conflicts with the management of the subsidiary. This argument can best be presented orally by a member of the seller's senior management who has cordial relations with the management of the subsidiary and who can state that he believes the subsidiary personnel were not entirely at fault and they are competent.

In far more cases than the participants realize or are ever willing to admit, the reasons for a subsidiary's difficulties, failures, and eventual sale are personality clashes and communications problems between subsidiary management and the management of the parent company. Most people in business understand this phenomenon, and there is nothing wrong with stating the fact when it exists. It can be presented that the parent company was able to take a broad view and still believes the subsidiary has real possibilities with the existing management regardless of differences. These debilitating communication problems usually occur between the management of the parent and its foreign subsidiaries. Proper presentation of this rationale can prove to be a very effective sale argument.

A companion rationale to personality conflicts is the one that, although relations have always been cordial, the seller has never truly understood the company, its market, or the country in which it is located, and has not been successful in contributing anything to it. In short, the company was unable to manage the subsidiary. This rationale is embarrassing and is best handled in an oral presentation. It is particularly effective with potential buyers who are strong in ego and possess a background in operating the same type of subsidiary as the one for sale. It is painful for a management to admit it is incapable of managing a company, but most sophisticated executives know there are limits to any management's capability and time.

Forced Sale

A never contested and always accepted rationale for selling is that the government is forcing the sale as a result of antitrust proceedings. A settlement with the Justice Department or a court order is something anybody can understand, and no further reasons for the sale need to be given. The seller can express his extreme disappointment at being forced to give up the subsidiary and explain all its virtues and reasons why he is selling with great reluctance. Divestiture for antitrust reasons requires no other reasons whatsoever, and the seller need not and should not give any even though he may have a number of valid other reasons for selling the company. In fact, he may secretly be delighted with the antitrust ruling. The seller's disadvantage in an antitrust ruling is the buyer's awareness that a sale must occur within a certain time limit which may or may not be extended. However, the buyer does not know how many other prospects are considering acquisition of the divestiture or what price they are willing to pay, and this may balance against the fact that the owner must sell before a deadline. Essentially the same basic conditions exist when the seller is faced with threatened or actual expropriation.

Liquidity Requirements

The seller needs cash. Here is a reason readily understood and perfectly acceptable. The seller can venture forth all sorts of reasons as to why cash is needed, or give no reason at all and let the prospects come to their own conclusions. However, it is better to give the factual reasons such as wanting to reduce debt, satisfy creditors, strengthen cash position for future acquisitions, increase product development, or generally improve liquidity. A public company particularly will find it necessary to explain the reasons for their desire for cash in order to avoid undue suspicions on the part of prospects and rumors that could affect the seller's share value. Public and private companies should use care in their "desire for cash" arguments not to unduly alarm creditors, unless the creditors are already worried and the divestiture program has as an objective their pacification. There are endless negative conclusions that a prospect and the public could assume in the absence of a valid presentation on the part of the seller. These could range from views that the subsidiary to be divested is worthless to suspicions that the seller is in desperate financial condition regardless of any published statements. The seller, public or private, should exercise care not to appear so desperate for cash that he will sell the subsidiary at an unrealistically low price.

Sale Caused by Poor Performance

The rationale that the subsidiary has failed for the seller and he has given up and wants out is what the buyer will believe or at least suspect regardless of any reasons given except that of an antitrust decree, expropriation, or desperate cash requirements. The tendency to sell only problem subsidiaries is so ingrained in the thinking of business executives that it will be most difficult to convince anyone to the contrary. Again, there is nothing wrong with admitting failure and stating that the present management has recognized its limitations.

The reasons for failure should be ascertained in detail and most can be conveniently categorized as mistakes, nonrecurring situations, or conditions beyond present management's control. By identifying causes for failure or inadequate performance, one is also identifying what can be done differently by a new owner in order to produce satisfactory results. The more the seller can identify specific decisions or problem situations that have been, are being, or can readily be corrected the more easily the sale will be accomplished. Product failure, inadequate estimating, noncompetitive prices, poor location, ineffective marketing, and obsolete designs are examples of specific reasons for poor performance that are readily explainable, possibly correctable, and can become cornerstones of the conceptual business plan developed to establish and justify price.

Minimum Return Objectives

Some corporations have policy objectives requiring all operations and subsidiaries to produce a minimum return on investment or pretax profit on sales. A subsidiary not meeting these objectives may be profitable and easily equal or exceed the performance of its competitors, but it still would not meet the objectives of the parent. A retail operation's percent of profit to sales, regardless of how well managed could not be expected to meet an objective set primarily for manufacturing companies nor would a metal fabrication manufacturing company in a highly competitive industry have a percent of profit to sales equal to that of a chemical manufacturer. For a company determined to apply its policy minimums to all operations, there is no alternative but to divest of those subsidiaries that cannot meet the objectives. This is a valid reason for sale and one prospects will understand, although they may openly or privately express their disagreement with the policy while conceding it is working to their advantage.

Sale to Stop Losses

The seller may wish to cut heavy losses and want out as soon as possible. This will be apparent upon the prospect's examination of the financial statements and the main area of discussion will not be why the subsidiary is for sale but how much of a one time loss will the seller take to get rid of it. A subsidiary with a record of unprofitable months will not be sold at or above book value unless it has greatly undervalued assets, which may be liquidated, or has prospects for a definite return to a profitable condition, which is most unlikely.

Capital Requirements

The subsidiary may either be profitable or unprofitable but there may come a point when it must have a substantial input of capital. This may be for further development expenses, new equipment, facilities, working capital, or for many other reasons to enable it to exploit its present position. The additional capital may be beyond the means of the owner and he will attempt to divest the subsidiary. Great care should be taken to accurately determine in complete detail the amount of additional capital required or the seller's estimates will be suspect. Unless shown convincing proof, a prospect will usually assume the amount of required new capital will be greater than that calculated by the seller. Sales for this reason are difficult because a buyer has two purchase obligations; one is for the business as is, which is a firm price, and the other is for the new capital to make the business a success, which is not fully known.

Loss of Confidence

One of the most difficult reasons for selling to present to prospects is the one where the owner has lost confidence in the subsidiary and becomes convinced it is a business without a future that will only decline. Technological obsolescence, government regulations, shifting markets, undesirable locations, and cost disadvantages can cause a business to have a bleak future. Such an outlook will hardly be encouraging to prospects and the seller should concentrate his reason for selling on limited specific reasons that can be remedied rather than a broad general loss of confidence. The seller's views may not be entirely valid and he will do well to call in outside consultants to see if they can develop a brighter picture of the future for the subsidiary under the direction of a new owner. The seller's representatives can also maintain this to be the view of the board of directors, but it is a controversial decision within the seller's organization with which all do not concur. Included among the dissenters are of course the sales representatives.

Reason to Buy

Regardless of all the reasons why the present owner has decided to sell, it is far more important to develop the economic and non-economic reasons why someone should buy the subsidiary for the price established. The emphasis in the entire sales presentation to prospects must be on why the prospects should buy and not on why the seller wants to sell. The owner's reason for selling should be treated as a significant part of the general presentation with the purpose of providing a logical introduction and lead-in to the reasons why a prospect should buy.

The reasons why a specific prospect should buy will be the results of the conceptual future business plan and constitute the critical part of the sales presentation. The conceptual business plan is described in Chapter 5, "Pricing." The plan will establish and justify the price and the seller must anticipate at some time in negotiations a prospect will request an explanation of how the price was determined. The conceptual business plan will primarily be economic, but intangible psychological factors should not be excluded from the sales presentation. Factors, such as the purchase will increase the prospect's overall status in the industry or increase the status and scope of authority of a decision-making executive are worth emphasis. Defensive factors, such as what happens if a prospect does not buy, should also be considered for tasteful presentation. The seller should avoid giving detailed financial projections to prospects but the business plan assumptions should readily be given since they will become an integral part of the sales presentation. While it is not advisable for the seller to give a buyer the detailed financial forecast, the forecasts should be in such complete and presentable form that they could be given without hurting the seller's case if the buyer insisted on receiving a copy.

The seller's position ideally should be that if the buyer makes the recommended moves of the seller's business plan, then he will receive an excellent return and will confirm this to be the case when he makes his own forecasts. The seller should state that his business plan or approach is only one way, and the buyer should be able to do even better. The owner should sell the concepts and assumptions of the conceptual business plan and then the financials will follow. A prospect using the assumptions of the conceptual business plan may very well develop financials more optimistic than the seller.

Tailoring the Sales Presentation

The sales presentation should be known to all involved and consistently presented, although reasons for buying should be tailored to each specific buyer for maximum effect. An experienced and perceptive executive managing the sales program can accelerate and improve the chances of the sale by making the sales presentation more effective through this tailoring process. This is done by placing emphasis on the arguments that will be most effective with a given buyer. None of the arguments are deleted, but they can be arranged and stressed in a more persuasive manner. Illustrative arguments demonstrating a synergistic effect will always be well received. It is unlikely that a seller's representative in meetings with prospects will have the opportunity to present all the reasons for buying and all the assumptions of the conceptual business plan at one time so he must have the mental agility and perception of the buyer to put forth those points that will make the greatest impression. By not providing a detailed financial forecast that would quantify the various arguments, the seller is free to vary his emphasis and thereby persuade the prospect.

The most persuasive arguments will be the ones a buyer readily comprehends and upon which he is able to place a value. He may not inform the seller of his calculations or place a low value on them for bargaining purposes, but he will only believe his own work. This tailoring of the sales presentation involves the utilization of all the data which has been accumulated about a prospect. An analysis of the data will enable the seller to prepare his sales presentation in such a way that each prospect contacted will feel he is receiving special attention and is not just one of many to whom the subsidiary has been offered. The stakes are so great in any divestment that a seller must fully plan his contacts on an individual basis.

Program Timing

Careful thought should be given to the timing of the commencement of the sale and the first contact of prospects. Once the decision is made to sell, there will be a desire to see the program start immediately, but it should not be started prior to the time it is well organized, the selling team is given their assignments, adequate data is accumulated, and executives are fully ready to begin definitive discussions with prospects. It is a major mistake to start the program before one is organized because the best prospects will normally be contacted first and these are not the ones to discourage with a poor presentation.

The question will also emerge in the sales presentation of "Why is the subsidiary for sale *now*?" A better question may be "Why wasn't the subsidiary put up for sale a year or so ago?" The seller may very well wish he had but at that time did not have the benefit of hindsight. The seller should be prepared with a candid answer. Most subsidiaries are put up for sale long after action should have been taken and the seller need not feel he made a unique mistake. Often because the subsidiary was a favorite of some key executive, nothing could occur until the executive was no longer on the scene or he was finally overwhelmed by financial conditions. Many companies are not accustomed to selling off subsidiaries for any reason and the decision to do so is long and difficult. Executives always hope things will get better or the latest medicine for the subsidiary in the form of a reorganization or management changes will save the patient and eliminate the need for more drastic measures. Whatever the reason for selling or the timing for selling, the optimum time has probably passed, but this need not trouble the seller. He should realize it no longer matters and just be prepared to explain his timing and get on with the sale.

Sales Program Preparation

Many prospects have been discouraged and sales lost because they found the seller did not know the subsidiary well enough to discuss it, or the financial data was inaccurate, inconsistent or confusing, or many small problems existed that could have been cleaned up to give a better general impression. Prospects should be made to realize they are buying an opportunity and not a mystery or a mess.

A realistic approach is to set a tight but adequate schedule for the accumulation of whatever data is required, preparation of the sales literature, preparation of the subsidiary, and finalization of the sales program. The schedule should be adhered to. Set a specific date for the first contacts to start. However, do not set a date that coincides with the expiration of a difficult union contract or the other operational situations where adverse results detrimental to the sales program could be occurring at the same time discussions with prospects are underway. How much time is required prior to first contacts will depend upon how much has already been accomplished, the amount and quality of manpower assigned, and the availability of those necessary for key decisions.

Inconspicuous Assets and Liabilities

Woven into the sales presentation will be information on the attributes of the subsidiary that are not readily apparent. Undervalued assets, valuable leases, employees with extraordinary talent, patents, assets written off but retained, favorable market conditions, large backlogs, and new products ready for introduction are examples of attributes not reflected on balance sheets that the seller should not be shy in presenting. All the liabilities of the subsidiary also need to be known, whether apparent or obscure; but they need not all be presented by the seller immediately or in some form of comprehensive list. They will emerge soon enough.

Handling Bad News

Bad news and subsidiary problems must be identified, and a strategy for their voluntary presentation or handling once discovered by the prospects must be evolved. The major problems that will be immediately obvious anyway to sophisticated prospects should be promptly presented in early contacts with the prospects. Early presentation before the prospect brings up a problem shows that nothing is being concealed and allows the seller to explain. As a general principle, a seller should always include the disclosure of a problem with an explanation for its existence and a solution. Explanations may include the problem was a nonrecurring event, it no longer exists, it is now being solved, or this is what should be done to eliminate it. If no solution exists, then the explanation will be that because of the problems the subsidiary's price is low. Open presentation of a problem tends to divert attention from others, and it is a good sales strategy to encourage a prospect to believe that with the solution of one or two obvious problems all will be well and this may turn out to be exactly the case. If the seller presents the major problems first, he has the opportunity to diminish their negative impact with his explanations and he can place emphasis on those which are least troublesome to explain.

There are no perfect companies, including those of the prospects and all have numerous minor problems or areas where they could be strengthened or improved. Minor problems need not be volunteered to prospects but the seller should be aware of them. Many conditions that the seller may consider to be problems may not be considered problems by a prospect.

Problems large and small emerge during a prospect's investigation that were unknown to the seller or the subsidiary's business may suddenly deteriorate in the interim after first contact but before closing. If the condition substantially affects the value of the assets, increases liabilities, or jeopardizes future earnings, then the seller may be forced to make price concessions to retain the prospect. However, the seller should not volunteer price concessions until he can assess how disturbed the prospect is by a problem's revelation. The prospect may not be troubled at all or may just walk away, but the seller should not be quick to reduce the price. Subsequent investigation may prove the problem to be of lesser dimensions than first thought or heretofore unknown assets or positive factors may surface that will offset the problem.

The unexpected surfacing of unknown problems or sudden earnings deterioration will be discouraging to the selling team and cause considerable embarrassment. Although they were totally unaware and surprised, they are placed in the position where it appears they were untruthful with the prospect. Their embarrassment may cause an unnecessary volunteering of concessions to the prospect all out of proportion to the consequence of the problem exposed. The seller's best position will be to express to the prospect astonishment at the turn of events, conduct an investigation, and then decide upon a course of action.

Presenting the Price

A portion of the sales presentation will be devoted to justification of the asking price. Thus justification should not be given a prospect in written form because a prepared statement would become the subject of frequent, close analysis and verification of assumptions and calculations, which would be counterproductive. A written statement also places the seller in the position of implying his stated reasons are the only reasons 'for the price. If a prospect can prove anything illogical or erroneous, the seller will have difficulty in maintaining his price.

The oral presentation of the price justification, which is by far most effective, is simply a candid summary of how the seller arrived at the price. This approach is so easy and effective in a divestment situation that none other is worth considering. The forces and factors that influenced the seller in setting the price will then all become supporting arguments for the price. The prospects may not be happy with the conclusion and will probably try to negotiate it down, but they will not be able to accuse the seller of taking an arbitrary and unreasonable position. This candid approach to price justification demonstrates to a prospect that the asking price is not just a price thrown out for bargaining purposes that the seller never expects to receive.

Final Considerations

Internal discussions relative to the possibility of divesting a subsidiary, as well as investigatory activities necessary to gather data to decide upon or prepare for a divestment, have a habit of becoming common knowledge. It is quite likely that some prospects may contact the company prior to the time the seller is ready to begin discussions. This puts the seller in an awkward position in which he is not ready to begin discussions but does not want to lose or discourage the prospect. The early prospect may not be the most logical or best prospect, but he is one who has a definite interest. At this stage, the seller may be unwilling to confirm publicly the subsidiary will be for sale nor does he want to be in a position of being untruthful with a valid prospect. The best approach is to simply inform the prospect that he will be contacted if and when a decision to sell is made. This should be adequate to hold interest, and during the conversation the seller can take the opportunity to engage in a general discussion with the prospect to better determine his degree of interest.

Subsidiary Access

Specific procedures need to be developed on access to the subsidiary's facilities by prospective buyers and how this access will be controlled. *Prospects should never be permitted free access to a facility.* They should always be accompanied by the senior representative of the seller, and at a minimum, the president or general manager of the subsidiary. Some prospects like to seek out information on a subsidiary entirely on their own and will employ all sorts of devious means to secure information and opinions. Explain to them that such is unnecessary. Prospects should be informed very early in the overall process that they will have access to the facilities and employees but they must follow established control procedures. A system of feeding the results of all visits back to one central point should also be established. Feedback data should be evaluated and placed in the individual prospect's file.

Supplemental Data

Procedures for securing additional date from the subsidiary will have to be established. An individual in the subsidiary who will be the point of contact for procurement of such data must be arranged prior to commencement of the outside contacts. No matter how much data has been secured in advance, the prospects will always think of additional data that they believe is needed. Whatever they want must either be provided or the prospect is to be given a full explanation why it is unavailable; otherwise, they will assume bad news is being concealed. In addition to the special project type data that will be required from time to time for prospects, a complete set of all new financial reports and copies of all internal reports of the subsidiary should be mailed to those responsible for the sale. Those responsible must continually be apprised of the exact condition and latest results of the subsidiary.

Prospect Contact

A sales program should include the tentative assignment of individuals to contact specific prospects and the sequence and timing of the contacts. This should systematically be accomplished by making a list of all prospects and then giving the assignments to those who can be most effective in making the contacts. These assignments should be made early to allow adequate time for the individual assigned to assimilate all the data gathered about a prospect, secure supplemental material, and structure his sales presentation for maximum effect.

Ideally, the person making the contact will know enough about the subsidiary and the prospect prior to contact and will have molded his presentation to the point where he is convinced the prospect will buy once he has all the facts. The reasons for buying and price rationale will best be presented orally, primarily in face-to-face meetings.

Sales Brochures

After determining approximately how the prospects are to be contacted, short and long form sales packages or brochures will have to be prepared and assembled. The sales packages are to provide standard basic information about the nature of the subsidiary and are not to be broadsided to prospects without further comment. At the minimum, the comment is a personal cover letter to the prospect's key executive that begins the process of explaining why the prospect should buy. It is best for a brochure to be handed to the prospect and all reasons for buying along with more details of the subsidiary woven into a convincing presentation. No other method of presentation compares favorably with that which can occur in face-to-face meetings. The number of sales packages to be developed will depend upon the number of prospects, but as a general rule one should develop at least twice as many sales packages as identified prospects because some will require several copies. Considerable care should be taken in developing these sales brochures.

One sales package should be a short form used to determine if there is preliminary interest on the part of a particular prospect. The short package will usually be given with a cover letter after telephone contacts, in general mailings attached to cover letters, and at meetings where the prospect shows only limited interest but does not unequivocally say no. The short preliminary package should include product literature if such is available, a description of the subsidiary including its history, basic activities and markets served, a list of physical locations, a brief description of any unusual assets or special features of the subsidiary that have obvious value, and an indication of size by stating the approximate sales volume or number of employees. Photographs of attractive facilities should be included. The individual in the selling organization to contact should be listed along with some description of the owner. Financial data or price should not be included in the short packages because the package's only purpose is to call attention to the fact that the subsidiary is for sale, give a general description of what it is, and create interest.

A much longer sales package should be developed for follow-up presentation to prospects who have received the short package and indicated interest. It may be given to prospects who have shown evidence of a strong interest in the subsidiary following brief discussions. The long package should include everything contained in the short package plus current financial reports, preferably audited, an organization chart, description of the competitive position of the company, and a list of patents of any other highly unusual assets. *Under no condition should projections or forecasts be included in any package.* Projections tend to come back and haunt the seller if the sale takes any length of time. The price should not be included in the sales package since it can better be given orally.

Both sales packages should have attractive but not gaudy covers. Their contents should contain whenever practical, standard readily available material and not include elaborate special presentations. If special pro forma financial reports are included, care should be taken to have in them ample notes so they readily can be compared with regular internal reports.

The purpose of the sales packages is to provide adequate information for a prospect at an early stage and should not be considered a complete and total presentation sufficient for the prospect to make his final decision. As discussions continue, the prospect will have hundreds of questions that could never be fully anticipated in a prepared description of the subsidiary.

Eventually a prospect will want complete financial information on the subsidiary, which will be verified by his own accountants or auditors who will expect full access to the subsidiary and its records. The seller must assume he will have to disclose everything at some time because a prospect will seldom buy if data is withheld. However, the timing of the release of financial data and its form in the early phases of discussions presents the seller with decisions that will be influenced by several factors. A seller will not want to disclose financial data to anyone other than prospects who are seriously interested but the prospects will not know the degree of their interest until they have some financial data. If the subsidiary has had poor financial results, then the seller will want to present the results in a manner that explains or mitigates the condition. The overall accuracy of historical financials may cause the seller to be reluctant to disclose this data, but accurate financials are critical to gaining the prospect's confidence and must somehow be developed. Taking these factors into consideration, the seller should include in the long sales package only *current* financials. If it is an autonomous subsidiary that is audited separately by a public accounting firm, then a copy of the past year's audited statement is ideal. A seller can attach an explanatory statement pointing out extraordinary events or other features that put the numbers in the best light.

Most subsidiaries will not have audited statements and some pro forma statements may have to be constructed. The best approach is to use the internal financial reports as a basis for the pro forma financials and add ample footnotes and explanations for clarification. The serious prospects will eventually review the internal reports, and they should not be confused with pro forma reports that cannot be readily reconciled to the internal reports. It is foolish to develop pro forma reports that delete loss product lines and extraordinary events, write up assets to market value, and make similar moves to improve their appearance. Point out the importance of such items in footnotes or other attachments but do not create statements a prospect will not believe.

Particular care should be taken to include in footnotes the amounts of any management fee or the effects of transfer pricing activities with affiliate companies. Nonrecurring or extraordinary conditions should be emphasized in accompanying notes. Division or product line financials should have ample footnotes to describe the nature of the operations. The only circumstances that would justify giving five-year historical financials in the long sales package is when these show an exceptional record of continual improvement that would be highly impressive. This normally is not the case in a divestiture. Some sellers try to withhold poor financial results in hopes of creating so much enthusiasm in a prospect for the subsidiary that he will buy it regardless of the financials. All this approach does is delay the day before rejection occurs and builds false hopes. Early disclosure of the bad news accompanied by an explanation or solution given in a face-to-face meeting with the prospect is the best approach.

Buyer Financing

Financing that may be available or can be arranged for a buyer need be evaluated and determined prior to making the actual contacts. The question of how much debt a seller will carry and what collateral will be required must be finalized, but if the seller can arrange for a buyer to be financed by others, then the seller will not only succeed in being promptly paid, but he will have added an attractive factor to his overall presentation. It is a powerful combination for the seller to offer both a subsidiary that could be highly profitable and the means of financing the purchase. In some cases, even if the seller had to guarantee the financing, he would be ahead to do so. Carrying the financing or arranging for third party financing will greatly increase the number of probable prospects because many are unwilling or unable to pay cash for a divestiture. If there are friendly banks, insurance carriers, private investors, or other institutions to finance such a transaction, then these should be identified. If a sale of assets was contemplated, then an industrial revenue bond may be available. All possible sources of financing should be ascertained prior to the first contact so the seller will be able to advise prospects of their alternatives. The ability to provide financing could mean the difference between success and failure in a divestment program and time devoted to this will be well spent. The seller should not take the stance that financing is only the buyer's problem.

As much as time permits, the entire sales program and the seller's position and decisions on each aspect should be reduced to writing and assembled into one or two volumes. A basis for such a written program can be answers to all applicable questions contained in Appendix C. Another volume containing all the data and answers to the questions in Appendixes A and B will also be helpful. Through a systematic gathering of information, highlighting of decisions, and organizing of the material into volumes, the seller will not only have a more organized and comprehensive program, he will have his material in convenient form for ready access.

9.
Prospects

A comprehensive list of prospects should be developed and ranked on the basis of their willingness and ability to buy the subsidiary. The ideal prospect is the one with the financial strength to buy who believes he can make the subsidiary more profitable and in whose short and long-range business plans the subsidiary fits. This prospect hopes to enjoy a synergistic effect or be able to defend his present position, or both if he acquires the subsidiary. In some situations, the prospects are easily identified and limited in number as would be the case in divestitures in the transportation industry. However, this is not the norm and a systematic and comprehensive program is necessary to identify prospects. The prospect list should be as all-inclusive as possible and include prospects who may appear only to be remote possibilities.

Once a prospect is identified as a possibility, more effort is required to evaluate the probability of interest through the use of available information. *Dun & Bradstreet* reports, annual reports, SEC reports, product literature, newsclippings, and any other data available on identified prospects should be accumulated. From these a general indication of the prospect's probable interest often can be ascertained. The published material should be supplemented by checking with those who have direct knowledge of a prospect. The seller will never know a prospect's real level of interest until he directly contacts him and presents the divestment opportunity. Material published about businesses is frequently inaccurate, and, even when accurate, it is out of date. While in many cases the published and third party information about a prospect may be suspect, it is all the seller has and it is far better than nothing at all for preliminary estimates of probable prospect interest.

The seller should ask himself if he is concerned with the general reputation and character of prospects. Prospects may emerge who have a reputation for sharp business practices, legal entanglements, or ruthless treatment of employees. Some sellers would sell to the devil himself while others will only sell to a prospect they consider worthy to deal with and to carry on the business. This is a decision each seller must make for himself. The decision will probably be influenced by how badly the seller wants to sell and if the transaction is for all cash at closing.

The larger the transaction, the fewer are the prospects. The subsidiary to be divested with a $50 million net worth will logically have very few interested and financially capable prospects and these should be readily identifiable. A subsidiary with only a million dollars in net worth will undoubtedly have many more logical prospects but of varying degrees of difficulty to identify. This fact that the number of prospects is inversely proportional to the size of the subsidiary to be divested should be kept in mind in developing the program and estimating its chances of success. The seller should limit time on prospects who have the desire but not the financial ability to complete the transaction, unless the seller is desperate to sell and willing to sell on a high risk, low cash basis. The prospect with low financial resources but great desire should never be totally discouraged because, if in time the seller is unable to find a stronger prospect, he may have to return to those only capable of an innovative transaction financed or guaranteed by the seller. The prospects capable of the larger transactions will more frequently have their aspirations complicated by government reviews and potential controversies with shareholders. Large prospects often have cumbersome internal bureaucracies that delay decisions, produce excessive evaluations, and in the end prevent acquisition of divestments unless the seller can secure the interest of the buyer's chief executive officer. Of course, problems of this type common to larger prospects may occur with smaller ones.

Sources of Prospects

As many people as possible should be brought into the process of identifying and evaluating logical prospects. It is helpful to give those assisting in prospect identification a list of prospect categories to remind them of the possibilities. Such a list frequently has a remarkable effect in helping those involved to recall likely prospects. Key executives, regional and division managers, and employees of the seller should be solicited for their ideas. Everyone involved in the actual selling program should be asked for their thoughts on prospects. The seller's public accounting firm and law firm may have suggestions. Some of the best suggestions will come from the employees of the subsidiary up for sale. They cannot normally be consulted until the decision is made to sell, but they can prove to be an excellent source of prospects. Rumors may have circulated concerning a sale, and the employees may have been contacted for confirmation by prospects. Individuals in the past may have inquired about the willingness of the parent to sell the subsidiary which the employees would recall.

Prospects can also be sought out systematically once their business activities are identified. For example, if the subsidiary for sale manufactures a certain piece of equipment that is primarily sold to specific industries, then companies in that industry can be identified through the *Thomas Registry* in the United States or publications such as *Kompass* in Europe. Sellers should look for prospects on an international basis rather than a regional or domestic basis. *Dun & Bradstreet, Moody's,* and *Standard & Poors* are helpful references. The editors of trade publications will help if requested and often possess valuable insight. Most industries have trade associations that can be contacted. Professional societies have available lists helpful in cases when the subsidiary for sale provides professional services. The seller may even place a blind advertisement in a leading financial publication such as the *Wall Street Journal* or the *Financial Times* in London. Such advertisements usually attract brokers but some prospects may respond.

Industrial Development Groups

Industrial development commissions that are primarily concerned with promoting new industry may be a source of prospects and aid vigorously when the alternative to sale is liquidation. Some commissions are extremely effective and have wide contacts, knowledge of industry, and know the identity of aggressive investors. They have extensive information on available public and private financing that could be an essential element in the eventual transaction. They also have area economic data on everything from wage rates to taxes, which prospects may want to inspect before making a decision. Such data takes on added importance when a prospect is evaluating the subsidiary as a base for expansion. A seller should be aware that there are wide variations in their levels of competence and interest in providing assistance, but their potential is so great it will be worth the seller's time to attempt to enlist their aid in the area where the subsidiary is located. Commissions of this type may be chartered at the ministerial level in a country, on a state or provincial level, regional basis, municipal basis, or even as the private promotion of a public utility.

Bankers and Creditors

The seller's or subsidiary's bank may be a source of prospects. The chances of the bankers knowing or finding any prospects is not high but it is possible they may produce some leads. If the seller is heavily indebted to the bank, then the bank should be informed of the seller's plans and, under such circumstances, the seller may as well enlist the bank's aid. Requesting their assistance is also a method of demonstrating that action is being taken to solve problems. Calls for assistance may bring more help and attention from a seller's banker than is wanted, and a company should first evaluate its overall relationship with their bankers before requesting such involvement. If the seller is greatly indebted to a bank, then the bank will have more incentive to aid just to protect its loan. In some countries the bank itself may be a prospect to buy. The banks may not produce prospects but they may eventually play a key role in financing a buyer and their prior involvement and interest may facilitate the financing.

Creditors often have a real incentive to locate prospects. In fact, a creditor may prove to be an excellent prospect. The subsidiary or seller may be so much in debt to the creditor and in such poor financial condition that takeover is the creditor's best hope for payment. Creditors must have at one time thought the business to be a good one or they would not have loaned it money or permitted it to become heavily indebted to them. Even in situations where the creditor's investment is not in jeopardy they may willingly assist. As in the case of bankers, there also may be psychological advantages in asking their assistance.

Foreign Divestitures

When the subsidiary to be divested is located in a country other than that of the parent, many special circumstances may exist. Each country will have its own set of conditions that must be evaluated, but there are some general observations that may be helpful. If the seller knows of one or more very logical buyers within the county where the subsidiary is located, then he may as well contact them directly and attempt to negotiate a sale. If he does not, then he should enlist the aid of the host government and local banks in seeking a buyer. The host government may buy or arrange a purchase of the subsidiary, because in many countries the banks are owned or under total control of the government and it can be expected that they will work together.

The government and banks will have a perspective unlike the seller but one not necessarily detrimental to a sale. They would like to see local ownership and may be more concerned with employment levels than they are with problems of the seller. In general their sympathies will not lie with the seller and they may be openly hostile to the seller. In disputes between the seller and a local national, the government can be expected to find a way to support its own citizens regardless of the merits of the seller's position. Prevailing political attitudes will preclude any other approach. Despite the government or bank's attitude toward the seller, they can see the sale as a means of furthering nationalistic interests and at the least an opportunity for rewarding political supporters or feathering their own nest. If the government or banks already own part of the subsidiary, they will be the most logical buyers.

Once the decision is made to sell a foreign subsidiary and no prospects are identified, then as early as possible either the host government or bank should be contacted. Governments do not enjoy surprises and usually are slow to react, so the seller should begin the dialogue as soon as practical and anticipate a long program. If there is an active relationship with a bank, start there and enlist their aid. If not, contact the government, which need not be initiated within the country. The seller can easily first present his problem to representatives of the host government at the embassy in the seller's country or at the United Nations delegation. They can get matters moving and, possibly, play a major continuing role themselves by identifying the best approach and appropriate channels within the country and arranging meetings with the proper individuals. There also is the advantage of using such contacts because they are readily available, have influence within their own country, and have a responsibility of sorts to further relations with the seller's government.

A divestiture of a significant subsidiary could easily become a major factor for good or bad in the relations between the respective governments. If the matter becomes public, the seller can assume the local press will take a hostile attitude toward the seller and be uninterested in the economics of the situation as it has affected the seller. Once it is a public issue, the government and banks will have much less flexibility to assist and act.

In divestiture of a foreign subsidiary, the parent should be careful to fully assess the relationship between the parent, the subsidiary, and the host government. What financial and technological guarantees has the parent extended? Can the subsidiary survive unrelated to the parent? Could the parent simply abandon the subsidiary? Are other operations of the parent dependent upon the subsidiary for parts or raw material? Are the subsidiary's problems caused by the host government, such as unrealistic import or export duties, excessive or confiscatory taxes? What is the attitude and policy of the host government both short and long-term towards majority or minority ownership by foreign nationals? Is the subsidiary's local management well connected with the government? What is the overall state of relations between the subsidiary and the government, public, labor groups and the press? Could the host government revise policies in such a manner that the subsidiary could become more profitable if new shareholders were brought in? Governments have been known to greatly modify policies in order to reduce or prevent unemployment and benefit local nationals and particularly when the new shareholders were political supporters, members of the government or their relatives.

Similar Companies

Related equipment manufacturers or service organizations should be considered as exceptional prospects. These are companies that are in related businesses and to which the product or service line of the subsidiary for sale would represent a logical extension of their existing capabilities. These prospects would understand the nature of the business and readily be able to grasp the advantages or disadvantages of the acquisition. They could visualize economies in combined distribution, the advantages of the combined or coordinated facilities, and the potential of interchange of personnel.

When the subsidiary for sale represents something of a missing link in a prospect's total line of services or manufactured products, then the subsidiary becomes very attractive indeed. Examples of this type of situtation would be the case of a pump manufacturer who had all basic types of pumps in his product line except turbine pumps or a process engineering company that had no capability in designing sulfuric acid plants. A manufacturer of wooden office furniture could have an extreme interest in a company that manufactures metal furniture. Extension of an existing line offers the opportunity for convincing arguments to be made to a prospect. This type of prospect is also able to quickly evaluate the situation and make up his mind. He may even have been considering the possibility before he was contacted.

Similar Distribution Companies

A general category of prospects are those selling to the same customers. The products or services of the subsidiary and the prospect may be totally unrelated but if the customers are the same, then it may be a viable situation.

Marketing costs are always a major area of concern, and if savings can be accomplished through partial or fully combined sales efforts, a prospect will listen. A subsidiary with a strong sales organization that could market more products would be a good match with a company in need of increased distribution capability in the same market. A subsidiary with a fine product but weak marketing group would fit well into a company possessing a strong sales group. The seller should systematically determine whom the subsidiary sells to and then find out who else sells to the same customers; and by this process prospects will be identified.

With any of these conditions, a prospect can perceive obvious advantages that will secure his attention and he will feel comfortable in the evaluation because he will not be on totally unfamiliar ground. He will be able to quickly assess customer attitudes about the subsidiary, which may or may not help the seller's case but it will hasten matters to a conclusion.

Manufacturers' representatives of the subsidiary either domestic or foreign may have an interest. Companies that distribute their products through independent organizations have this group of prospects to evaluate. Often these independent marketing companies are more prosperous than the manufacturer and over the years have built strong companies of substantial worth. They have a dependence on the manufacturer for a supply of products, proven ability to sell it, and frequently strong opinions on how the manufacturing operations could have been run better. Marketing oriented people tend to underestimate manufacturing problems and vice versa. Should the subsidiary be involved in marketing primarily, then the manufacturers would be prime prospects.

Suppliers

Suppliers, either domestic or foreign, could conceivably have an interest because they can readily see the acquisition would allow them to control and possibly increase sales. In some cases, they may look at the acquisition as a defensive necessity to protect their existing sales. Competent purchasing managers attempt to develop a number of suppliers for any particular item, and consequently a supplier would have competitors in providing the requirements of the subsidiary. An acquisition would enable the supplier to provide 100% of the subsidiary's needs. From a defensive standpoint, a supplier could be quite concerned about retaining existing sales and fear that a sale of the subsidiary would result in subsidiary personnel or policy changes that could affect his status as supplier. To them a sale to another competitor could have disastrous consequences.

Prospects need not be limited to existing suppliers but should include all potential suppliers. Those on the outside trying to get in may have even greater incentive. Suppliers also have the added advantage as prospects in that they have some familiarity with the business to be divested and will have less difficulty in understanding and evaluating it.

Licensors and Licensees

Licensors and licensees represent viable prospects. They may have a major interest in seeing that a stable relationship exists between themselves and the subsidiary. They may also believe the relationship could be improved and expanded if they were to control the subsidiary. In some cases, the relationship may be so critical to the prospect that he has little choice but to go ahead and buy the subsidiary. Adverse financial consequences could occur if the subsidiary fell into the hands of competitors, creditors, or others who would wish to modify the relationship.

Licensing agreements frequently contain provisions describing the rights of the parties in the event the subsidiary is sold. Agreements should be carefully reviewed to determine the nature of such rights, if any; and their existence may provide the opening basis for negotiations on the acquisition of the subsidiary by the other party to the license. When language of this type exists, conversation with the other party becomes a necessity in order to consummate the sale with anyone; and this conversation may as well lead into the subject of their buying the subsidiary. If they decline to buy, they will be in a position where they can object less about another buyer.

In the same general category of licensing are franchise operations. If it is a successful one, then the issuer of the franchise is a prospect or other successful franchise holders are prospects.

Customers

Customers and clients are a possibility. Concern over assuring an adequate source of supply is always a major consideration in a well-run corporation, and the opportunity to have captive suppliers is attractive to many. Obviously their degree of interest will be influenced by the total of present sales and whether or not suitable alternatives exist. Manufacturers of private label merchandise will find it particularly productive to look to their major customers as prospects. Many large distribution and retailing organizations have moved back into areas of manufacturing by acquiring suppliers to assure a reliable source. In addition to present customers and clients, potential customers and clients should be treated as prospects.

Former Shareholders

Former shareholders or owners of the subsidiary may be excellent prospects. These people would be familiar with the business and in all probability believe they could again run the business very well. In fact, they may still be the management of the subsidiary. These former shareholders may have adequate funds to make the acquisition. They may still own some stock of the selling organization and be willing to trade all or a portion of that stock to secure the return of a subsidiary they created. If not interested themselves, they may prove an excellent source for identification of other prospects. They may recall other suitors from the period of their ownership. Former shareholders who previously ran the subsidiary successfully may have such credibility that they would be financiable with a high leverage type of deal.

Joint Venture Partners

Joint venture partners of the subsidiary will be logical prospects and in most cases agreements already exist whereby each partner has rights of first refusal if another desires to sell. These are people who would be interested in maintaining a stable relationship and would have a general knowledge of the subsidiary's business. They would know the personnel and the industry and its markets thus permitting a speedy evaluation. A successful joint venture normally involves a considerable amount of association between key executives of the respective partners, and this would provide the opportunity for contact and discussion of the situation. Chances are that in such a situation conversations could be conducted on a most confidential basis. Joint venture partners with other subsidiaries of the seller should also be considered as potential prospects if the relationship is good.

Employees

Employees of the subsidiary will want to buy it, but they seldom are able to come up with the necessary money or credit to complete the transaction. Frequently employees of the subsidiary for sale have little concept of the subsidiary's worth, and they lack knowledge of the amounts of working capital required to make a sizable operation function properly. They also may assume the seller is unaware of the subsidiary's value because of what they perceive to be the seller's lack of support or poor past management decisions. Employees will always be a prospect in the category of those who would take on a transaction if financed, primarily by the seller. They can be looked at as buyers of last resort.

Employees may also be the most logical prospects to acquire a small subsidiary where a major sales effort could not be economically justified or the owner did not have the capability to conduct a sales program and wanted a quick, private sale. Sales of this type may be tantamount to abandonment with the seller having a low probability of recovering his investment, but conditions may exist that justify such a transaction.

Care should be taken in discussions with employees so as not to create embarrassment by belittling their chances. Tell them, if they can come up with the money or required financing, there is no one the seller would sooner see buy. Care also must be taken to secure a defensible market price from the employees in order to avoid charges of a sweetheart transaction and stockholder suits.

A financing arrangement that has been worked out with employees is the vehicle of an employee stock ownership plan, commonly called ESOP. With ESOP plans, the employees' pension fund purchases the business, and the pension plan is ultimately compensated through profit sharing contributions made from the future profits of the acquired company. ESOP plans are fairly complicated, but they can be accomplished and are becoming increasingly popular. Under ESOP plans, both principal and interest payments on the debt are tax deductible. ESOP plans have also been tied in with certain government funding programs designed to assist minority groups or businesses in distressed areas. There are problems connected to ESOP plans with the largest being the necessity to retire the debt from profits that may not occur in every year over a 10 to 20-year span of time.

The seller should be careful not to become too deeply involved with employees unless there is a high probability of actually completing a transaction with them. There is no point in getting their hopes high only to tell them "no" at a later date because of the lack of available financing. In a sale to employees, the seller will normally have to provide the sophistication and expertise to consummate the transaction. Owners should be alert to the possibility of subsidiary executives and employees conspiring to cause a deterioration in the subsidiary's performance or presenting the subsidiary to prospects in a manner that would drive them away and thus improve their own chances of acquiring it.

The subsidiary management may want to purchase the subsidiary and transactions of this type do occur. Financing is again the big problem and challenging but often highly leveraged financing packages are available to managements who appear competent. Most are done on the assumption that the executives will work harder and better as owners. The lenders and the seller will do well to evaluate the validity of such an assumption and not engage in rationalization in their zeal to dispose of the subsidiary or put together a deal. Any transaction with employees or management will be complex but can be worth the effort.

Competitors

Competitors are possible prospects, but the seller should be extremely wary in dealing with competitors. Most will claim an interest in acquiring the company, but their degree of seriousness is problematical. The temptation to get an inside look at a competitor is nearly irresistable; and even though a competitor has no interest in purchasing the subsidiary, he will frequently pretend and take the opportunity to investigate the subsidiary and secure ammunition to use in his own sales program. Of course it can be a two-way street, and a clever seller may learn more from the competitor while he is discussing and evaluating the subsidiary than the competitor will learn from his efforts. The seller can learn much general market information and the names of other possible prospects. Serious prospects will have many questions about competitors and direct information about them can be very helpful. Although the seller chooses not to deal with competitors as prospects, he should obtain as much information about them as possible, including D&B's, product literature, and SEC reports if they are public.

Antitrust problems are always possible in contacts with a competitor, and, in large transactions, antitrust regulations may prevent the acquisition unless it is a "distress sale." Exchange of pricing data during the evaluation process can also produce unpleasant government action. A competitor does have great opportunity for gain through acquisition of another competitor, because it is equivalent to the elimination of a competitor. Combining similar operations has obvious inherent economic advantages and the resultant larger organization would have greater influence over market conditions and pricing factors. Many countries have laws to prevent such results and a seller should not make any moves with competitors without legal advice. However, in some countries, mergers of competitors and practices inconsistent with a free market are permissable.

Similar businesses that are not competing because of geographical factors are exceptional prospects. In these cases, prospects will know and understand fully the business. Chances are key personnel in the subsidiary and in the prospect's organization are already acquainted with each other through various trade association meetings. Industries where this type of prospect would be particularly prevalent are retailing, distribution, warehousing, and transportation including barge lines, airlines, and railroads. In these cases, an exchange of personnel is readily possible and economies may be accomplished through combinations of facilities and reductions in overhead structures.

Lesser Prospects

Companies specializing in the parts or service fields may have an interest in the subsidiary if it is a business that is relatively old and its markets are declining, but a substantial long-term business in repair parts and service exists. This is a specialized field that can be quite lucrative for those who know and understand the parts and service business. A sale to a company of this type may be the best way for a seller to meet legal and moral obligations to continue to provide parts and service to past customers.

Certain companies are composed entirely of divestitures from other corporations. A review of the portfolios of these firms normally reveals they will buy any type company and are not overly concerned with how a subsidiary fits with what they already own. They make a practice of buying divestments and have the management skills to handle problem situations and absorb the companies. They usually are able to quickly evaluate subsidiaries, make decisions, and are skilled in negotiating and financing such transactions. Here the problem may lie for the seller in that the negotiation may be an unequal contest. The buyers probably will have considerably more experience in buying and tend to only accept deals that they believe to be certain successes for them and the price is a "steal." They can readily assess the seller's position and need to sell and drive a hard bargain. Also, because of their reputation as buyers, they are continually being offered other opportunities so they know if they lose one, there are many others to look at.

A promotional type company whose copious publicity is only exceeded by the ego of its chief executive officer may prove to be an excellent prospect. Companies of this type are extremely growth oriented. They are interested in acquiring anthing they can lay their hands on that will support the promotion of their stock and give substance to their arguments of being a dynamic growth company in a particular field.

Wall Street thrives on fads such as it has on computer software, recreation, pollution control, and energy; and there are always marginal companies quick to perceive and capitalize on such phenomena. These companies can be readily identified by reading the popular business press where stories appear describing their business activities and demonstrate the effectiveness of their PR departments. Acquisitions in the field they are touting tend to give credibility to the promoting firm and impress the investing public. Should a company tout itself as an environmental engineering group, then a company in waste treatment would be very attractive. A company specializing in discount retailing would find retail stores in other geographical areas attractive. Care should be taken by the seller to secure cash, and he should avoid accepting stock, unless it is promptly marketable, or notes, unless well secured, because these companies do not always survive for long periods.

If substantial real estate is included, consider the owners of the adjacent property. They may want the property so much that they would pay the premium of acquiring a going business to acquire the property. Should the two businesses be at all compatible, then this becomes an even more likely prospect. Whenever the real estate has a market value greater than the business, separate sales of the two should be considered.

Minority holders of stock in the subsidiary could prove to be prospects. This situation does not exist in many companies, but, where it does, a large minority holder would represent the prime prospect. The minority holder's role is not always a happy one, and the availability of the majority shares would provide the opportunity to take full control of the company. If they have no interest in acquiring the balance, a concerted approach whereby both the minority and majority holders were offering to interested prospects 100% of the stock, would provide a better alternative than offering less than 100%.

Conversion of a 100% owned subsidiary into a joint venture is a prospect that can be attractive and have many advantages. In some cases, it is possible to sell a portion of the subsidiary to a group that could bring into the subsidiary advanced technology, management, distribution, or other benefits it presently lacks. This option is attractive to foreign prospects because they can become involved with a relatively low profile and have access to the knowhow of the seller. If the subsidiary is foreign based, some prospects may want to acquire an interest as a means of entering into business in the country where the subsidiary is located. These joint ventures with domestic or foreign investors can produce many benefits other than those directly associated with the subsidiary. A close association with a responsible group can provide the means for creating other joint ventures, financing assistance, or business opportunities.

Sale of a part interest and the creation of a joint venture can be a first step toward a complete sale because joint venture agreements usually contain buy-sell provisions that establish the means for a complete sale. Differences in operational approaches can hasten the implementation of the buy-sell terms or encourage the new participant to seek another partner to take out the other. Should either party to the venture want out and the other refuses to buy them out, they still will find it necessary to enlist the other party's aid because prospects will not buy into a hostile environment.

"All others" is a category not to be slighted. One never knows with certainty where the best prospect will come from, and it may come from nowhere and for no apparent logical reason. As the sales program progresses and it generally becomes known that the subsidiary is for sale, this type of unexpected and unsolicited prospect seems to automatically appear. These are prospects who do not fit into any of the previously described categories. They may simply be those who are interested in expanding into new areas of the type the subsidiary represents. They may also be people with money who are looking for a suitable investment. It would be a most unusual sales program if during its course some totally unexpected prospects did not emerge. No amount of research would have identified them prior to their contacting the seller.

A sales program will also bring to the surface promoters of no substance, big talkers, con men, and the like. The seller should be very cautious with private investors or individuals who claim they can raise money or have the money available to make an acquisition. When dealing with private individuals, regardless of who they say they are or what the seller may believe he knows of them, it is only fair to demand references and proof of financial ability before discussions go too far. Reputable prospects are willing to provide proof of financial ability and adequate references. Those who cannot produce such should not be seen again.

The seller should be on guard against prospects of dubious ability to buy and make a point of quickly assessing their ability and interest so as not to waste time and disclose data to those who will not buy. However, the seller will be wise to meet with all prospects who contacted him at least once. The seemingly unlikely prospect may prove to be the excellent one who eventually buys the company. A seller will seldom be in a position where he has such an abundance of serious prospects that he can arbitrarily afford to disregard any without a direct evaluation.

The preparation of files on all the prospects should be accomplished as early as possible, and lists of all prospects in order of importance should also be developed for handy reference. This material will become the basis for maintaining control of the program and insuring proper, adequate, prompt contact and follow-up.

10.
Final
Preparations

Most activities to prepare a subsidiary for sale represent good business practices that should be followed regardless of a sales program. These are practices designed to improve the appearance of the subsidiary, eliminate, reduce, or define the scope of potential problems that would surface in negotiations, reduce the total investment in the subsidiary, and revise as required the ownership of assets or the entire subsidiary. A reduction in total investment will either increase the profit on the divestiture or make a price reduction possible. Strong management and in some cases, special programs will be required to implement the practices; but, because of their obvious desirability, there should be minimal resistance other than that caused by the usual lethargy and shortage of time.

Positive activities associated with cleaning up the business and elimination of long-standing problems will have a desirable psychological effect on the employees. Employees will tend to take more pride in the operation, feel more like a part of it, and realize they are contributing to an overall sales program that could favorably affect their future. Various steps and programs designed to optimize the condition of the subsidiary prior to and during the sales program should commence as soon as the decision to sell is made.

Legal ownership of the complete subsidiary, assets, and liabilities must be reviewed and, when appropriate, transferred to make title consistent with the method of structuring the sale and to take advantage of tax provisions. If the sale is to be treated as an offshore transaction, then the subsidiary should be made a subsidiary of an offshore company if it is not already one. If patents are to be separated, then the patent ownership should be transferred and licensing agreements developed. If a subsidiary is to be split up with part retained, such as the marketing, and other parts placed up for sale, then extensive planning is required.

Subsidiary Appearance

The physical facilities should be maintained in the best possible condition consistent with the financial resources of the seller. A few thousand dollars' worth of paint may be one of the best investments the seller could make to consummate a multimillion dollar sale. Minor repairs, which are obvious but easily accomplishable, should be rapidly completed. Furniture that is badly worn should be disposed of or moved to less conspicuous locations. Particular care should be given to reception areas so they are in a presentable condition. All of the lights should be in working order and burned out bulbs replaced to avoid the drab impression of a poorly illuminated area. If the roof leaks, have it repaired. If it is a manufacturing plant or warehouse, then lines on the floor should be repainted. In offices, a policy of everyone totally clearing off their desk at the end of the day will do much to bring about a more orderly appearance. If it can be accomplished tactfully, employees should be encouraged to look their best. In general, an overall housekeeping improvement plan should be instituted. The more bright, cheerful and businesslike the facilities can be made to appear, the more attractive they will be to a buyer as well as having a salubrious effect on the morale of the employees.

A strong program of neatness is particularly important if the subsidiary has been in an unprofitable position. All too often in losing companies there is a reluctance to make even the smallest of expenditures to maintain a neat and orderly appearance. Such facilities develop a "smell of death" appearance. If there have been major cutbacks in personnel, an office will look better if total sections are closed down rather than having large numbers of desks sitting empty in many rooms and locations. The same applies to manufacturing operations where, if possible, it is better to close down total departments or bays rather than have only a few people in each one. Generally, it is more efficient if employees are working reasonably close together and are not spread out at great distances. A program to improve overall appearance does need to be tempered by good judgment and should not be overdone to a point where it looks as though the seller is attempting to deceive the prospects.

An important element in the clean-up activities can be the overall safety program that a manufacturing operation usually has functioning. General housekeeping is a major part of any safety program, and whoever is responsible for safety could be given the instructions and backing to see that a superb job is done. The safety engineer or other individual responsible will undoubtedly welcome the opportunity to perform a first class job. At the same time, all other safety hazards should be eliminated. Prospects will demand the results of the latest

OSHA inspections and expect to see compliance before they buy. Many prospects will rank the quality and results of a safety program as key indicators of the competence of management and their level of performance.

All scrap material and waste should promptly be removed and sold. Every business creates waste but in manufacturing and production operations, excessive amounts of scrap and waste material rapidly accumulate unless a vigorous program of prompt disposal is maintained. Offices also generate substantial quantities of waste that should be removed. In addition to removing scrap accumulated daily, a complete facility search for all scrap and waste material should be conducted to rid them of material that has been lying about for a long period of time. In little used buildings or on the grounds surrounding the buildings large quantities of waste material and scrap can often be found which should be disposed of to improve the appearance and hopefully be sold at a profit. Maintenance departments are great for accumulating unnecessary waste material on the assumption that they never know when they may need a particular item. During a vigorous clean-up and scrap disposal program, it is far better to follow the general principle of "when in doubt, throw it out." If there is little chance of the excess material being needed in the immediate future, it is best to dispose of it. Another advantage in the scrap disposal program is that it will produce some income. This will be immediate income to the current owner; while if the material is sold with the business, the seller can be certain that it will not bring one additional penny in price.

Government Relations

A review of the subsidiary's compliance and relations with all government agencies should be conducted and any deficiencies, non-compliance orders, or disputes should be resolved. The multitude of agencies that can and do regulate business is so large that it would be impossible to mention all, but special attention should be given to EPA, OSHA, IRS, and the Wage and Hour division of the Department of Labor. Resolution of differences with bureaucratic agencies can be frustrating and time consuming so work should commence early.

Excess Assets

Unused office machines, machine tools, real estate, general equipment, vehicles or other superfluous assets should be disposed of prior to the sale. Care should be taken not to sell assets that are currently needed in the business or will be needed during a modest but imminent expansion. The disposal of superfluous assets will generate income for the owner and have little or no effect upon the price to be received unless the assets are of great value or the excess assets were promoted to the prospects. A buyer is primarily interested in the business and will not be concerned about the disposal of the excess assets if he was told they were excluded and in most cases will be happy to see them gone and out of his way.

If excess assets are not readily disposable, they may be transferred to other locations of the seller. At a minimum, their title should be transferred to the parent company or another subsidiary in the event their disposal is not completed prior to the sale of the total subsidiary. It is a desirable objective to have all excess assets sold or removed from the subsidiary before it is shown to prospects. Once a prospect sees an asset, he will assume it is included in the sale unless informed either before or at that time it definitely is not. An asset may be excluded initially from the sale but included at a later time as a bargaining concession.

Receivables and Retentions

Receivables should be closely watched and every effort made to resolve problem accounts. Coupled with the clean-up of slow accounts should be a program of additional diligence on the part of those who are responsible for granting credit and are in a position to prevent problem receivables. A list should also be made of the receivables written off in prior years, and all should be reviewed to determine if there is any possibility of collection. Receivables are certain to attract more than their share of attention during the negotiations because of the uncertainty of their collection and the question of whether or not reserves are adequate. The best way to reduce the scope of this area of negotiations is to reduce to the lowest possible point the number of outstanding problem accounts. Customers or clients who may have been given more time and leeway in the past should be promptly pursued. A special directive should be given to the individual or individuals responsible for granting credit and for the collection of problem accounts to exercise greater persistance and caution.

Receivables often include retentions. These are amounts held back by customers or clients until work is performed satisfactorily, equipment is properly functioning, or a plant is performing at the agreed specification level. These may be uncollected for reasons ranging from no one asked for the money to withholding of funds because of customer dissatisfaction. Whatever the reason, the amounts should be promptly resolved and collected if possible. Any outstanding will be a warning to buyers that a problem exists.

Inventory

Reducing inventory to the lowest possible level is a desirable business practice and appropriate for a subsidiary about to be sold. The better the overall quality of the inventory the better the subsidiary will appear to be run and the more attractive will be the balance sheet. Special programs should be initiated to eliminate surplus, obsolete, and slow moving inventory. The inventory reduction program can be greatly assisted by restrictions on the purchasing operations in order to prevent more coming in the front door than is going out the back. Previously written-off inventory should be disposed of. Written-off inventory will contribute nothing to the price to be received for the subsidiary, and any cash received prior to the sale of the subsidiary can be retained by the seller. Excessive or low quality inventories are readily apparent to trained observers, and these same observers will be impressed by an absence of undesirable inventory. The number of turns of inventory in the course of the year and the amount of excess, surplus, or obsolete inventory are indices of the quality of management, which will not be overlooked by a sophisticated prospect. In the eventual negotiation, the burden of proof will fall upon the seller to fully substantiate the book value represented by inventory. He need not complicate his task by having an "unclean" inventory and one with which he is unfamiliar. Should any of the inventory be in the distribution system on a consignment basis, strong efforts should be made for its control. Special promotional programs are usually warranted to encourage its sale.

Contract Review

Contracts and agreements of all types should be reviewed to see that they are still valid and applicable to the present conditions. Agreements that have been in effect for many years should receive special attention. Often formal agreements expire with both parties still satisfied with the relationship, and it continues on although no written contractual relationship exists. This condition is common with sales, license, and supply agreements. A new owner could constitute a change the other party would find unsatisfactory and in the absence of a firm agreement, decide to terminate the arrangements. A program to review and bring current all contracts should be completed prior to sale.

Records Retention

A program of records retention, records destruction, and key record duplication must be carefully planned and initiated. There are legal requirements that specify the minimum length of time records must be retained, and in most cases the minimum period is a reasonable maximum time to maintain records. If such a program does not exist in the subsidiary, then the program should be set up and implemented immediately. The seller should remember that once the sale is consummated all the records of the subsidiary sold will normally go to the buyer and be in his possession unless other arrangements are made. If there are records in the subsidiary that the seller wishes to retain, then these should be removed or at least duplicated and transferred to another site. In most areas, companies exist that specialize in the storage of duplicated or little used records. These companies can also be of assistance in setting up record retention programs. Unless the seller retains possession of all records, he will be wise to insist upon language in the sales agreement that gives him full access to them.

Litigation

Pending litigation should be resolved if at all practical. If it is not practical to resolve the litigation, then the seller should at a minimum have the best expert advice as to its probable outcome in order to plan his negotiating position with prospective buyers. Buyers are reluctant to become involved in situations where uncertainty exists. In most cases where the subsidiary is the defendant, the buyers will insist on protection against losses in one form or another. Litigation is difficult to accelerate, and it seldom will be speeded up unless the attorneys are urged to do so. However, there is no point in pushing the litigation if it would increase the probability of loss once the final award or compromise is reached.

If the seller retains responsibility for the litigation, as is frequently the case, then he has incentive to see the litigation concluded prior to sale. To try a case would normally require the subsidiary employees to be witnesses who may or may not be willing and effective. As long as the seller retains control of the subsidiary, he will be able to have some control over the witnesses. Once the witnesses work for another company, which has no responsibility or financial stake in the litigation, they easily can lose their interest. For most people, even under the best of conditions, being a witness is not a pleasant prospect and they will not go out of their way to participate.

Warranty and Service

Product warranty problems should be resolved in as expeditious a manner as possible, but this does not mean undeserved claims should be paid. Product warranty obligations again will be a difficult issue in the negotiations, and the buyer will be sensitive to any liability. The fewer the claims outstanding or threatened the less will be the seller's exposure. Once the subsidiary is sold, the seller will be dependent upon his former employees for assistance in resolution of claims for which he retained responsibility, and these employees may not provide willing assistance. Complete information on significant warranty claims prior to sale is a necessity for their resolution and to protect the seller.

Stabilize Workforce

Termination and replacement of marginal employees in the subsidiary should be avoided because most prospects will prefer a stable workforce. This is particularly applicable for conspicuous members of the management group. The employee that existing management and the seller consider to be of low competence may be the very man that looks best to potential prospects. Furthermore, opinions developed about the competence of a particular individual may be unduly influenced by one or two incidents of which only the seller is aware. Often the marginal employee is one who has been employed for a long period of time, and he is not good enough to promote or bad enough to fire. The termination of such an employee may lead to an adverse reaction from the other employees. If the seller was able to live with this particular employee for a good many years, it will not be easy to understand why the relationship could not continue until the new owner took over. Chances are it could without any difficulty.

Supply Agreements

The subsidiary should avoid long-term commitments with suppliers unless the benefits from the commitments are extraordinarily advantageous. What may appear to be an advantage to the present owner may be no advantage at all to a new owner. Of course, during abnormal periods of extreme material shortages, long-term supply commitments to the subsidiary can be an added inducement for the buyer. In most cases though, the buyer prefers to have the flexibility to make his own decisions.

Open Disputed Matters

The overall program of final preparations should result in the resolution of most disputes but usually not all can be concluded on a prudent basis prior to sale. The cost of settlement may be too great or moves to settle may indicate weakness, which would adversely affect a potentially fair settlement. It may be premature to even consider settlement because of inadequate information and the need to accumulate all the facts. Full information about open disputes or conflicts will be vital for the negotiators and those responsible for formulating proposed contract language. The system should not be such that those working on the problems are not communicating with the negotiators. This communication process should continue on a regular basis throughout the sales program until closing occurs. It will enable the negotiators to know the points about which they should be flexible or firm and which areas they should avoid entirely.

Communications

Prior to launching the contacts with various prospects, there should be final meetings with operating management and parent company officers so that everyone is fully informed of the program and has an opportunity to ask questions, understand it, and criticize. There are so many facets to a sales program that constructive criticism can always be helpful. This is an undertaking where seldom is there one right way to do anything but there can be several right approaches that have an equal chance of success. Meetings to discuss the entire program will be particularly helpful in eliminating conflicts between various groups that develop during programs of this type. They provide an opportunity for a general understanding to be reached as to what the program is all about and also to learn that it is an unequivocal company policy to proceed with the program.

At these final meetings, it is possible to generate many good suggestions about prospects, how to improve the sales program, and how to improve the operations and give it the best possible appearance.

A policy of full communications to employees and others directly involved is necessary. The company's law firm and public accountants and bankers should be kept informed. Most important, the employees should be kept fully advised and told how it will affect them personally. Divestment programs create many rumors, and the methods of promptly handling the rumors need to be developed. Usually it is a case of explaining that in all probability the sale will have little effect upon them. They will not believe this totally, but it usually turns out to be the case.

11.
Contact
and Follow-Up

Upon completion of the preparatory work, the planning, the proper notifications and approvals, the critical part of the program involving contact and negotiations with prospects can begin. The first contacts should be with the most probable prospects and continue on down the list to those of lesser probability. Prospects who had asked the seller if the subsidiary was for sale before he was ready or those who evidenced interest when the seller was "testing the water," would be among the first to be contacted.

If one or two highly logical prospects stand out from all the others, they should be contacted first and told that it is the seller's belief that they would or should have a serious interest and are being offered the subsidiary before others are approached. Such a presentation will imply to the prospects that with prompt action on their part they will not have competition. Absence of competition is a strong inducement for a high-probability prospect to promptly begin serious investigation and negotiations, but they should be warned they will enjoy their noncompetitive position only as long as they vigorously pursue the situation.

If the one or two prime prospects are contacted without success or no such prospects exist, then the next five to ten most logical prospects should be contacted within a one to two-week period. The seller should guard against becoming discouraged by slow or a low percentage of favorable responses to his sales presentation. This is normal and to be expected when one considers the magnitude of the decision a prospect is being asked to make. Slow responses are common and should not be interpreted as favorable or unfavorable in the absence of any other information. At this stage, the seller must assume the word is out that the subsidiary is for sale.

When contacted prospects decline or are slow to respond, new prospects should be activated to maintain a substantial, active group. Contacting prospects on a basis of declining order of probability not only accelerates the sales program, but it tends to minimize the problem of over-shopping. Buyers are reluctant to acquire subsidiaries that have been offered to others if they are aware such offers have been made. They tend to assume subsidiaries offered to and rejected by many others are not worth acquiring and they would look foolish if they considered the subsidiary. They fear they would be wasting their time because others could move faster or they believe they may be walking into an unwelcome bidding contest. Limiting the number of prospects with which the seller is having active discussions is also necessary because of time limitations.

One of the objectives of the sales team is to make each prospect feel he is given special attention because of the seller's tailored arguments that the acquistion of the subsidiary would be a great opportunity for the prospect. It is a bit inconsistent for the seller to promote this psychology and then be unavailable to meet at the prospect's convenience because of commitments to other prospects.

The selling team should avoid showing the subsidiary to two prospects in the same day and make all arrangements in such a way that prospects do not come in contact with each other. The management of the subsidiary, who the prospects will want to meet, does not have unlimited time to spend being interviewed. The management's primary activity must be to continue running the subsidiary, and their greatest contribution to the sales program can be strong optimistic leadership, effective management, and profitable or improving operations.

Perfecting the Presentation

Another advantage of spreading out the first contacts over a period of time is that with each sales presentation of the subsidiary the selling team will learn the weak and strong points of the program and which are their least and most effective arguments. This enables improvement in presentations to subsequent prospects. Regardless of the extent of preparations, unforeseen problems can develop in the presentation, and an alert selling team, looking for ways to improve, will continue to perfect their presentation from what they learn.

Prospects will indirectly assist in improving the presentation because they will be quick to identify weak points in the business operations or business plan of the subsidiary in their belief that it will improve their bargaining position should they become serious buyers. Most prospects enter into an acquisition investigation with emphasis on discerning and informing the world of what is wrong rather than what is right.

It may develop that certain individuals on the selling team are un-suitable for the project and should be replaced. An employee in the subsidiary to be sold may make a negative impression, and he should be avoided in the future or at least be advised on how he could help rather than hinder the sale. Undervalued assets or outstanding at-tributes of the subsidiary that deserve emphasis may emerge. The business plan for the subsidiary may prove flawed and have to be revised. The selling team with each improved presentation will gain confidence and learn how to concentrate the sales presentation on matters of most interest to the prospect. In a sales situation, it is com-mon for the sellers to believe all the subsidiary's warts are enormous and unduly exposed and to suspect everything that can go wrong will go wrong. This may be the case, but the seller should not forget the potential buyer has no perfect companies or employees because they do not exist. The task of the seller despite any problems is to emphasize the virtues, show how difficulties can be eliminated, and present the opportunity in the most convincing manner possible.

How and Who to Contact

First contact with prospects should be on a straightforward, dignified basis appropriate for a major transaction between organiza-tions or individuals of stature. Immediately prior to the contact all available information on the prospect should be reviewed to enable the seller's representative making contact to give the most impressive presentation possible. If only one or two prospects have been iden-tified, extremely thorough preparations should be completed before contact. The seller's representative should contact the prospect, state his purpose, and request an early appointment at which time he would make his complete presentation. Gimmicky or humorous ap-proaches are hardly fitting for this type selling.

The seller need not be shy or hesitant about approaching any prospect and, indeed, an aggressive program has no room for reluc-tance or shyness. The worst a prospect can do is say no, but most will be curious enough to want to learn more. After the members of the selling team make a few contacts, they will discover prospects are usually interested and courteous and whatever shyness existed will disappear. Often prospects who have no interest will volunteer the identity of other prospects or may even offer to assist in contacting others.

Determination of the individual who should be contacted at each prospect is an important decision. There is no question of who to con-tact if the prospect is a private investor or subsidiary employees, but most prospects will be corporations. Determining who should be contacted is not an easy decision and one of which the seller can never be certain until he knows the results. The proper person to contact is the most senior executive with rank and status who will give serious consideration to the proposal and could become a powerful advocate. This should be an executive who would understand the subsidiary and has the time to consider it or will assign its review to a subordinate but assure follow-up. The ideal contact will be an executive who is familiar with the industry or market of the subsidiary and may have had prior contact with the subsidiary or at least be generally familiar with it. The prospect's executive who allows the proposal to sit on his desk or in some subordinate's office indefinitely constitutes a difficult obstacle. His inaction can easily lapse into a negative, face-saving response unless supplemental contacts persuade him to act.

Should the chief executive officer of the seller be familiar with the chief executive of the prospect, then a direct approach between the two is the only proper approach and other contacts could be offensive. Any acquaintanceships between key executives of the seller and the prospect should be exploited to determine the proper channel and to enlist their aid in full consideration of the divestment. If the proper executive to be approached in the prospect's organization is totally unknown, then this individual may be identified by a telephone call to the secretary of the chief executive officer. The problem can be described, and the seller normally can learn from the secretary who would be the executive to contact. Secretaries frequently give the seller insight into the structure of the prospect's organization and advice on how best to proceed with the presentation. They are willing not only to indicate who should receive the presentation but also give information on how it should be presented—either by mail, telephone contact, or by a direct personal visit.

In a sizeable corporation, where the seller has no insight, contact may be with any of the following: the chief executive officer, the chairman or president who is not the chief executive, the planning or acquisition department head, or an assigned executive who looks after acquisitions, such as a semiretired chairman of the board. Another possible contact is the divisional operating manager, responsible for a large division to which the divestiture would be logically assigned and be highly complementary. Eventually, the chief executive officer will become involved if the prospect is seriously considered, but the planning department or executive assigned responsibility for acquisitions may be offended if they do not first process it. The same "nose out of joint" phenomenon can apply to the operating manager responsible for the complementary division. The seller has no certain way to avoid this type of intercompany conflict.

Some chief executive officers will want to be familiar with the situation very early but others, without review of any kind, will automatically refer the information to the department or individual responsible for preliminary evaluation of acquisitions. Often their secretaries send the material as received to those responsible for review and the chief executive never sees it.

If the operating manager to whom the divestment would be assigned if purchased is running an extremely profitable division, his opinions will be respected. However, if he is responsible for a problem division, he probably has little interest in acquisitions and his opinions will not carry much weight. The attitude of the executive to whom the subsidiary will be assigned if acquired is important enough to justify meeting him early in the sales program so he can be persuaded to favor the acquisition. He may not make the final decision but a negative attitude on his part will almost certainly kill the sale. The chairman or president who is not chief executive officer may be wondering about the nature of his job duties and be looking for activity and would welcome an acquisition prospect to evaluate and advocate.

In balance, the best approach when no one is known in the company is to determine if there is an executive responsible for acquisitions and make contact with him. If no such individual exists, then the chief executive officer would be the best approach. The operating manager will usually only be productively contacted first in large corporations where he is a rising star. The seller will have to do his best to assess the situation on the information available and then take his chances.

Methods of Contact

There are several methods of contact with the prospect. The most effective are face-to-face meetings, when information on the subsidiary is presented and an opportunity for discussion exists. The cost, time, and effort involved in individual presentations will easily be justified with a higher proportion of favorable results. Face-to-face meetings also provide the best opportunity for the seller to impress the prospect by giving his complete sales presentation. Most corporations receive many unsolicited acquisition opportunities and it is essential for the seller to have his efforts receive full attention and not be treated in a routine fashion. There is no substitute for individual direct selling where a perceptive seller in face-to-face discussions can tailor his presentation for the maximum effect and best assess the prospect's interest and the probability of a sale.

The second best approach is a telephone call to the selected executives in which the subsidiary is described in general terms. Then, assuming there is some interest, either a short or long sales package is promptly mailed to the executive with a personal cover letter referring to the telephone conversation, which contains a summary of the reasons why the prospect should buy. A telephone call will at least build some rapport, distinguish the seller's proposition from all the other unsolicited acquisition possibilities, give the seller insight into the prospect, and secure a preliminary indication as to whether or not there is any interest. If a large number of prospects are to be contacted and the selling team is small, then the telephone call plus the mailing approach is more practical.

The mailing of the sales package without a telephone call or a face-to-face meeting is the least effective. If such mailings are used, they should go directly to the chief executive officer with a cover letter utilizing information known about the prospect and giving a summary of why the prospect should be interested. Mailings of this type are only justified when a very large number of prospects are being contacted or because of special situations associated with the sale. Large mailings would only be appropriate for small subsidiary sales. The objective of mailings and telephone calls remains securing an opportunity for a face-to-face meeting.

Devious, indirect, and subtle approaches in which a third party informs the prospect that the subsidiary may be for sale are a waste of time; and they can work to the detriment of the seller. Such approaches may temporarily fool the prospect, but their true nature will eventually surface. Once they are exposed, the prospect may be offended and negotiations jeopardized. There is no practical value in such an approach because much more can be accomplished with a direct, straightforward presentation. This does not mean the aid of mutual friends should not be enlisted, but they should mainly be used to arrange meetings, with the subject known to the prospect in advance. Assistance of this type can help the seller receive a satisfactory hearing of his sales presentation.

The seller should maintain complete records on all contacts with prospects along with the file on each company. The files should contain copies or a record of all material given to a prospect. Those making the contacts with the prospects should be required to prepare detailed reports of the conversations and results, which would be circulated to the selling team and others interested, with copies placed in the prospect's file. Periodic summary reports on the prospects still active should be developed and circulated within the selling organization to those directly involved and as a part of management reports. A periodic report of the status of discussions with each prospect will also serve as a reminder to the selling team for follow-up purposes.

Follow-Up Activities

The seller can be too aggressive in his sales approach and destroy a portion of his bargaining position or antagonize the prospects. Most prospects have formal and informal procedures that will be followed and no amount of telephone calls, visits, or entertainment will accelerate or circumvent the procedures. However, the seller should operate on a basis whereby he is always waiting for the buyer and never a case where the buyer is waiting for the seller. If the buyer requests more data, then the seller can assume nothing will happen until the data is received. The quicker the data is delivered, the more promptly negotiations can start or resume. If the buyer wants to meet the subsidiary management and visit the facilities, such should be arranged without delay. By very prompt provision of pertinent data, services, or conveniences the buyer may want, the seller can keep the buyer in a position where it is always his move without becoming a nuisance or giving the impression he is desperate to sell.

The seller's representatives must be available to respond promptly to the wishes of the prospect and should take advantage of every opportunity for personal contact. The more contact possible with the prospect, the easier it is to build the proper rapport and the more likely the seller will develop an understanding of the needs, requirements, and problems of the prospects. The seller should continually be in the position of implying without saying, "What can I do to help you come to the conclusion I have reached that you would be wise to buy our subsidiary at our reasonable price?"

Once the seller has made his first contact, he should assume the sales program is public knowledge. It has been previously stated that it is impossible and unnecessary to keep a sales program a secret. This does not mean that what is going on should be broadcast to the world, but the seller need not be overly concerned when the information does become public knowledge. Regardless of what kind of rapport the seller may believe he has with a possible prospect and the nature of any assurances received, he should assume information given to the prospect including financial data will not remain confidential. The prospect will make copies of material received for internal use and soon copies will be made of copies. The seller must decide it is more important to sell the subsidiary than it is to keep data confidential and when his data suddenly is found to be in strange hands, he should resign himself to the fact and make no effort towards its recovery. Divestiture programs always offer prime commercial gossip, and most executives love to talk of these situations with their cronies. The gossip does have an advantage in that unknown prospects may hear of the subsidiary being for sale and contact the seller.

Dealing with Brokers

Once the program is underway and word is out of the divestment activity, business brokers will learn of it, contact the seller, and request permission to offer the subsidiary to prospects they claim as clients or volunteer to seek out prospects. The decision on the use or control of brokers should have been made before this time. With a vigorous program of direct contact of likely prospects, brokers are largely unnecessary and when approached, the seller can reject their services. However, a broker may appear claiming to know an interested prospect who is not on the seller's prospect list. The seller should explain to the broker that while willing to meet his prospect, the broker must look to the prospect for his fee and add that this should be no problem if the prospect has the claimed degree of interest.

The seller should be very careful not to inadvertently grant a broker an exclusive right to sell the subsidiary or the opportunity to claim a fee. Under certain conditions brokers can and do claim fees although no written agreements are in effect. If a broker can show that he arranged contact between the buyer and seller either directly or indirectly, he may be able to demand a fee. The best defense against unwanted broker fees is to immediately decline their services when offered and confirm the refusal in writing. Any arrangement with a broker where he may be entitled to a fee from either the buyer or seller should be reduced to writing to avoid misunderstandings.

Unexpected Prospects

Out of nowhere may come totally unsolicited prospects of whom the seller was unaware. The seller could not possibly have knowledge of all prospects and should respond initially to each as though he were a fully qualified buyer. However, very quickly and before written data is given to the prospect, he should be investigated to confirm he is as claimed and has adequate financial resources. No seller can afford to throw away prospects out of hand and even if information adverse to the prospect is turned up, it is worthwhile to confront the prospect with the data and learn if he can refute it. Chances are he cannot and will go away. The investigation may also show the prospect to be an excellent one. Buyers of substance will not resent a review of their credentials.

Meetings with Prospects

Many prospects will be quite unsophisticated in buying companies. The seller should not be surprised or offended if they do many things that appear strange, particularly in the course of the evaluation phase of reviewing the subsidiary. Prospects will not rely totally on information received directly from the seller and tend to prefer data that is secured from others and confirms data already received. They will conduct market surveys contacting customers, trade associations, and trade publications for their opinions. They will arrange for their representatives to meet subsidiary employees to solicit their opinions using a variety of ruses ranging from foolish to ingenious. A wise seller will be particularly sensitive to learn very early in his meetings with the prospect the degree of sophistication the prospect has in buying companies. This can be readily determined by asking how many companies they have acquired in the past or by asking as tactfully as possible how much experience the executives involved have had in buying companies.

One can assume that negotiations will go slower with a prospect unsophisticated in buying and the seller will be required to do a superb job of presentation and leading the prospect by the hand if the sale is to be consummated. One offsetting factor is that unsophisticated companies are more likely to pay unsophisticated prices and be slightly more subject to sales presentations rather than rely on cold evaluations. An inexperienced seller may also produce negative effects upon the proceedings.

Entertaining Prospects

Entertainment of prospects can be limited to dinner checks and modest refreshments. The people involved in evaluating divestitures and those executives making the key decisions usually travel so much and are so accustomed to living reasonably well that their decisions will not be influenced by lavish entertainment. Overbearing and demanding entertainment can have a negative effect. Obviously, poor hospitality can also have an adverse effect and should not occur. The seller will be wise to remember that a serious prospect is busy and mainly interested in learning the facts and making up his mind. Of course, in those cases where a prospect hints he wants to see the town, show it to him. Gifts should not be given, but if the subsidiary manufactures an inexpensive product or even an unusual part, prospects who visit the subsidiary should receive a sample. An item of this type that ends up in their offices is a constant reminder of the opportunity.

Status of Buyer and Seller Representatives

As much as possible, personnel of the seller should meet with the equivalent rank or status personnel of the buyer and preferably of relatively equal ability. A senior executive of the seller should always attend meetings with the president or chief executive officer of the potential buyer. In meetings involving only presentation of financial data to the buyer's accountants, it is best to limit it to an accountant to accountant basis. One type of situation to particularly avoid is where the seller is represented by a man of much greater status than that of the buyer. These people will have difficulty communicating, and it will appear the seller is desperate. The seller can assume that the buyer's interest will be reflected by the stature and level of the executive assigned to meet and discuss the possibility of buying.

Internal Power Structure

In meetings with a prospect, it is best to try to determine his internal power structure and procedures for making decisions. Even when the buyer is a single individual, the seller should attempt to determine if he has personal advisors upon whom he relies. Knowledge of the formal decision and approval structure is necessary but it is far more important to learn the informal system, which individual's opinions have greatest weight, and who will ultimately make the decision that all others in the buyer's organization will accept. There is no reason for the seller not to ask outright their procedures for making a decision and the nature of the internal power structure.

By equating who is involved and which stage the buyer is at in his internal procedures the seller has some idea of what must transpire before rejection or negotiations commence. Enormous amounts of time and energy can be saved by finding out early just how the prospect goes about making his decisions. A clever seller will use this knowledge of the buyer's structure to tailor his sales program for greatest effectiveness. The prospect may be so unsophisticated in making acquisition decisions that the chances of going ahead are negligible in which case the seller must either assist and educate the prospect to establish a system and time table or give up. The amount of money the buyer is spending in time, travel, and evaluations is also a good guide to level of interest.

Lost Prospects

Good prospects will seldom be so abundant that a seller can afford to lose any needlessly. A series of questions should be asked once a prospect says "no": 1. Could the seller's presentation have been made differently and more effectively? 2. What is the prospect's real reason for declining? 3. Is the executive saying "no" the final authority or can he be bypassed? 4. Is the negative response a bargaining position? 5.

Can solutions be found to the prospect's objections? 6. Can the prospect be revived and what should be the timing for moves to resume discussions? Upon notification of rejection, the seller should critically review his contact with the prospect and all that has transpired to determine what if anything he has done wrong. Once rejection has occurred, the chances of reviving the prospect are low but the seller can engage in introspection and learn to improve his performance and the odds with others. From this activity some real benefits may emerge if the seller is willing to take the harsh, and often unrealistic, position that the prospect was lost because of errors made by the seller.

Prospects frequently give a reason for declining that is not their true reason or only a lesser reason among many. The seller should evaluate the reason given against what he knows about the prospect. If it is totally logical and the refusal was specific, unequivocal, and from a senior executive, then little more should or can be done. If the reason seems superficial or inconsistent with what is known of the prospect, efforts should be made to learn the true reasons, which could lead into a reactivation of discussions. A usually successful ploy to accomplish this is to request a meeting with the prospect for the purpose of securing his opinions of the subsidiary and constructive criticism about the sales presentation. Most prospects are flattered and quite willing to participate in a program whose agenda can be expanded to include a discussion of the reasons for his rejection. The meeting will also be an opportunity to learn if the rejection represents a decision by the chief executive officer or some lesser official who made the decision without much thought or without policy guidelines and who could possibly be bypassed with a direct appeal to the chief executive officer or a board member. Such an appeal has to be carefully prepared and usually should be on the basis of presenting new or additional data which changes the picture rather than stating or implying the subordinate executive made a mistake.

Meetings to learn the true reasons for rejection can also be tactfully arranged or conducted by third parties or mutual friends. Once the true conditions are ascertained, the seller can evaluate his position and decide what if anything can be done to reactivate the prospect. This activity must include solutions and responses to the prospect's objections, the timing for presentation, and the wisdom of reactivation in light of the seller's overall objective and alternatives.

Negotiations

Eventually a prospect will conclude he would like to own the subsidiary and is willing to pay the asking price or some lesser amount and final negotiations can commence. A successful program is largely hard work and preparation and if the seller is well prepared, the negotiations should be relatively easy and almost anticlimactic. The well-prepared negotiator will have such a complete understanding of the business of the subsidiary for sale, its markets, and current financial condition that he cannot be surprised by any information thrown at him by the prospect. He will have in mind his own objectives and know his limitations.

The seller's negotiator will learn all he can of the buyer and look for the buyer's problem areas and objections and attempt to resolve or provide solutions or attractive offsetting factors. He will continually strive to look at the transaction through the eyes of the prospective buyer.

Much has been written on the so-called art of negotiations—some are helpful in a limited way and some expound inapplicable or poor advice. However, a divestiture negotiation and sale has certain characteristics that preclude most so-called negotiating tricks or techniques. The transaction is complex; it will be reviewed by experts, evolve over a period of months, and include at least two primary negotiations. One is for a letter of intent containing the basic terms or an oral understanding of the basic terms and another for a definitive agreement. Possibly other peripheral negotiations will be required with finance organizations, creditors, governments, leasors, and the like.

The negotiating concept that the buyer is the enemy and anything goes to get his name on the dotted line is total nonsense in divestiture negotiations. The principal negotiators have to develop a working relationship that will last for months and this can only be accomplished in a spirit of working together with a common objective for the benefit of both parties. So-called high-pressure selling won't work because there is no dotted line to sign that is legally binding for several months after agreement is reached on the basic terms. The buyer has ample time to reconsider and his initial decision will be reviewed by associates, lawyers, accountants, and various other real and self-proclaimed experts. Although as a general rule, the fewer the negotiators and the smaller the size of negotiating meetings, the better; two tiers of negotiations and negotiators usually develop in a divestiture. At the top level are the two principal negotiators for the parties who settle the basic issues, such as price and terms and all other issues that are not resolved by subordinates or the professionals. The lower tier consists of subordinates, lawyers, and accountants who are preparing and negotiating the definitive agreements and arranging for the transition of ownership. Skillful use of the lower tier of negotiators by the principal negotiators permits communication and resolution of differences that would be difficult if only the top negotiators were involved.

Options

Some prospects may ask for an option or the exclusive right to investigate the subsidiary for a set period of time. While this may be advantageous for the prospect, it is against the best interest of the seller unless he has no other prospects whatsoever in sight. Once the seller has his sales program underway, he cannot shut it down or suspend it for a particular time without running the risk of losing his other prospects. The sum of money adequate to compensate the seller for the loss of prospects and suspension of the program would be too large for a prospect to pay for an option. An option is only of value if it spells out the complete terms of purchase and this would be difficult without some investigation on the part of the prospect and full negotiations. Consequently, an option is not practical and should not be considered. If a prospect insists, he could be presented with the proposition whereby he immediately enters into a complete purchase agreement with earnest money and unless he finds the subsidiary substantially misrepresented within an agreed number of days, the transaction becomes final. Few prospects would agree to that alternative.

Options of any sort are seldom necessary because a prospect who diligently pursues his investigation actually has an informal option, which is as good as the speed with which he can move. This fact should be explained along with a statement of the seller's policy that he will not remove the subsidiary from the market until a satisfactory letter of intent is signed.

Letter of Intent and Transition

Although not absolutely essential a signed letter of intent is usually the first objective of the negotiators. It normally is not legally binding because it only covers the basic overall terms and is subject to the results of the buyer's audit, an investigation of the subsidiary, approvals of boards of directors, and, in some cases, shareholders and governments. It will include the agreed price, terms of payment, date of closing, and other points the parties consider important. While not legally binding, it is a mutual agreement that the prospect will buy unless unforeseen developments occur and the seller will sell on the agreed terms and not negotiate with others. Neither party should be satisfied with an oral agreement and both should want and insist upon a signed letter of intent. Once it is signed the seller should make every effort to see that closing occurs as soon as possible but realize this will be extremely fast if it occurs within six weeks.

The quicker the closing, the less time there is for things to go wrong, but it takes time to draft and agree upon definitive legally binding agreements, for the buyer's accounting analysis and audit to be completed, the buyer to arrange his money, and the board of directors to meet. If the buyer and seller are from different countries or in anyway the transaction is international, the time between initial agreement and closing will be longer because of different business methods, government approvals, language, and travel problems.

During the period after signing the letter of intent, the seller should not relax but keep right on selling and do all he can to totally convince the buyer he is about to finalize a wise decision. Now is the time when a good rapport between representatives for the seller and buyer is most important, a time for the seller to be stressing economic and noneconomic arguments for buying but with heavy emphasis on the noneconomic. If the seller has not confined his sales arguments to economic ones in the early phases of his relationship with the buyer, it will be easier now to stress the supporting noneconomic reasons for buying which are less subject to change than the economic ones.

If part of the inducement to buy is the possibility of a broad continuing relationship between the buyer and seller involving other aspects of their businesses, such as a new joint venture, licensing, cooperative buying, introduction to clients and key customers, or the seller becoming a customer of the buyer, then action should be taken to commence these activities before closing occurs if at all practical. A developing close relationship on a personal basis between representatives of the buyer and seller will also greatly help to bring about a closing. These activities can further convince or enmesh the buyer into the transaction and help overcome unforeseen problems that may surface prior to closing. Unexpected operating results of the subsidiary, new negative revelations about its condition, and disputes over terms of the definitive agreement can produce tense moments and possibly jeopardize the transaction. During this period the buyer's auditors will arrive determined to find everything imaginable wrong with the subsidiary and "protect" the buyer. A clever seller may have held back and not disclosed a few favorable aspects of the subsidiary knowing full well nothing warms the heart of an auditor like his personal discovery of undervalued assets or understated income. Carefully planned "discoveries" can also appeal to the baser instincts of the buyer. Until the final agreements are signed, the seller should not totally disband his sales organization and throw away his sales literature. He should do what can be done to preserve his alternative prospects.

Upon signing the letter of intent, the seller must assign a senior executive to act as a project manager to coordinate the employee and public announcements, legal, financial, and transitional matters to see that all is completed on schedule. Ideally this is the seller's chief negotiator but it can be someone else if he does not have time. This will prove to be a very time consuming activity.

Other prospects who have not responded or are delayed for one reason or another need not be contacted and informed that a letter of intent has been signed. When they do contact the seller, they should be told of the situation, be informed the transaction is not final, and they will be notified if it falls through. Prospects who had scheduled visits to the subsidiary must be promptly told of the turn of events and their meetings cancelled. To go through with previously scheduled meetings would be interpreted as an act of bad faith by the buyer and could jeopardize the transaction. The seller should not go out of his way to inform prospects unless such is necessary to prevent direct action on their part, but a timely candid explanation is a way of maintaining a spark of interest.

Multiple Prospects Bidding

Occasionally a fortunate seller has two or more prospects who want to enter into negotiations at the same time. A multiple bidding or auction approach is almost impossible, but a comparable technique may be used. Each prospect is informed of the existence of other prospects and given a letter of intent with key items such as price and terms left blank. It is important that they all have the same letter of intent to ensure that they are all bidding on the same thing and bids can be compared. They are told whoever bids the highest by a specified date above certain minimum levels will have the first opportunity to negotiate a definitive agreement. Should the high bidder fail to follow through and promptly negotiate the definitive agreement, then the seller can open negotiations with the second highest bidder.

Conclusion

When the day for closing the transaction finally arrives, both parties will be satisfied or they would not be there, although they are probably somewhat exhausted from the ordeal. For the seller, parting with a subsidiary may be a happy or sad event, but for those individuals who conceived, planned, and executed the sales program, it will at least be an event marking the accomplishment of one of the more difficult programs in business. The seller should hope the best for the buyer and if the buyer is able to exceed all his forecasts or resells the subsidiary at a later date for a profit, the seller should be happy for him.

Appendix A.
Minimum Data
Required to Decide

This list represents the minimum data required to decide preliminarily if divestment is a feasible course of action. In most cases, substantially more data is available or can be secured without great effort or exposure of the contemplated program. Ideally all information listed in Appendix B should be secured.

1. Most recent, unaudited monthly statements.
2. Most recent audited statement.
3. A list of nonrecurring or extraordinary charges for the past three years.
4. Conservative forecasts for balance of year plus two years forward. Carefully define assumptions for forecast.
5. Estimated gross profit on large jobs in-house and general condition of such jobs.
6. Statement of parent's investment in subsidiary. An amount needed to break even in a sale. Tax effect must be known.
7. Conservative cash flow forecast for balance of year plus two years forward. Define assumptions.
8. List of known problems in the subsidiary and the possible solutions to each along with cost, time, and ease of accomplishment estimates.
9. List of major strong points of the subsidiary.
10. What share of the total market does the subsidiary now enjoy? Is this growing or declining and what is the outlook? What is the total market?
11. Who are the major competitors and what is the condition of their business, their prospects for growth, and their share of the market?
12. What capital expenditures will the subsidiary require during the next five years?

13. How does the subsidiary's level of productivity compare with competitors in the country and outside?
14. Description of quantity and quality and backlog.
15. Description of attitude of banks and creditors.
16. Description of attitude and policies of government toward the subsidiary and those which would affect a divestiture. What are the government's policies on employee layoffs and termination pay?
17. What union and social factors would be significant in the event of a divestiture attempt.
18. If the subsidiary is foreign, what are the regulations on profit repatriation?
19. How would any other subsidiaries or operations be affected if the subsidiary is sold?

Appendix B.
Data Required Before
Contacts are Made

This is the data most commonly requested by prospects in a comprehensive evaluation of a subsidiary. The evaluation process will be expedited by having the data prepared in advance and readily available. The seller's representative should be familiar enough with the information to intelligently discuss the subsidiary with prospects.

1. All data listed in Appendix A.
2. Five years audited financials.
3. Recent copies of monthly financial reporting package sent to parent company.
4. Confidential evaluation of actual value of inventory.
5. Confidential evaluation of receivables versus book value.
6. The amount of inventory by location and inventory method.
7. Copies of all current internal reports of subsidiary to be sold plus arrangements for continual receipt of such.
8. List of all retentions held by clients and date and probability of collection.
9. Copies of subsidiary's budgets or profit plans.
10. An organization chart without names and one with names.
11. List of all salaried employees and their salaries. A list of salaried employees with titles but without salaries.
12. Copies of employee benefit plans.
13. Copies of employment contracts, if any.
14. Biographical data on key managers.
15. Copies of union contracts.
16. Summary of history and general description of current state of labor relations.
17. Description of each facility owned or leased and the number of employees at each one. Photographs of facilities if possible.

18. A list of patents, licenses, and franchises. Royalty payments made and received. Summary of age, termination and transfer provisions. Copies of all important agreements of this type.
19. Plant capability brochures or U.S. government form 251 for engineering companies.
20. List of major machine tools if manufacturing plant.
21. List of leases and summary of their contents. Have copies of key ones available.
22. List of vehicles, watercraft and aircraft, estimated value, and indication if owned or leased.
23. Copies of any recent appraisals of assets.
24. Estimate of the total capacity of plant or operations and current level of activity as a percent of total possible.
25. The advertising agency and a description of the advertising program.
26. List of sales personnel, their locations, and their annual compensation showing base pay and total compensation.
27. A 3-year sales analysis showing geographical distribution of sales—a breakdown by major categories and the profitability of each line.
28. Description and value of merchandise placed on a consignment basis.
29. A list of major customers and amount of purchases last year.
30. Copies of sales incentive plans, if any.
31. Copies of sales representative agreements, if any.
32. A list of major suppliers.
33. Names of any new products or services.
34. Product literature.
35. List and summary of all existing or potential litigation and evaluation of exposure or recovery.
36. OSHA inspection reports and status.
37. EEO reports and status.
38. EPA reports and status.
39. IRS audit reports and status.
40. Summary of relations with any government agency affecting the subsidiary's operations.
41. Summary of insurance coverage including loss experience, names of carriers, and annual premiums.
42. List of accounts or other accounting policy data that would enable a prospect to define cost of sales, gross profit, SG&A, etc.
43. Copies or summaries of major contracts with customers, an analysis of their status, and estimate of results.

44. Copies of summaries of contracts subject to renegotiation and estimate of probable results.
45. Secure ages of all major assets.
46. Statement on availability of energy of all types for the subsidiary and cost of energy consumed during past year.
47. List of all local and state taxes due or paid during the past year.

Appendix C.
Executive Checklist

In light of the fact that this book is intended to be a working guidebook to corporate divestment, this appendix contains synopses of all the chapters.

Chapter I
Divestment Alternatives

1. Before deciding to sell, the seller should determine his objective.
2. A study should be conducted to see if the objective could better be achieved by pursuing alternative courses.
3. The basic alternatives to divestiture by sale are:
   — retain the subsidiary and
      (i) improve operations
      (ii) run on static basis
      (iii) run and phase down or out
   — liquidation
   — shutdown and "mothball" facilities
   — take the subsidiary "public"
   — divest by issuing subsidiary stock to the shareholders of the parent
   — bring in new shareholders
   — abandonment of the subsidiary
   — any combination of the above
   — any combination of the above and divestiture by sale
4. To compare the alternatives with divestiture, the seller should estimate:
   — the price which realistically could be received for the subsidiary
   — the probability of finding a willing buyer
   — the time necessary to complete a sale

5. The seller should verify that he fully understands the subsidiary, its business, environment, and make certain all his data is accurate.
   — secure the data of Appendix A
   — secure the data of Appendix B

Chapter 2
Major Potential Problems

The owner contemplating sale must review the following areas:

1. The terms of all agreements with banks, bond holders, debenture holders, and other creditors.
2. The rights of common and preferred shareholders.
3. Obligations to a government for benefits received.
4. The extent and terms of all parent company guarantees for the subsidiary.
5. Bargaining obligations with a union representing subsidiary employees.
6. Obligations to former shareholders under "earnout" provisions.
7. Restrictive employment agreements.
8. Can the seller take the time necessary to sell the subsidiary?
9. Does the subsidiary have critical customer or supplier relationships with the balance of the corporation?
10. Will divestiture of the subsidiary create a competitor?
11. Are assets of the subsidiary leased and, if so, what are the terms of the leases?
12. What will be the nature of the corporation remaining after the sale?
13. What are the political implications of a sale for the executive involved?
14. Will there be a government or public reaction to a sale? How will it be handled?
15. Must the decision to sell be disclosed because of security law requirements?
16. Will there be a shareholder's reaction? How will it be handled?
17. What are the terms of licensing or marketing agreements of the subsidiary? Are there any restrictions?
18. What will be the tax effects of a sale?
19. Has a search for hidden liabilities or major liabilities of an uncertain magnitude been conducted?
20. Does the seller have the resources and determination to conduct a sales program?

21. What governmental, judicial, or regulatory agency review and approval is required?

Chapter 3
Major Questions Requiring Decisions

Decisions are required in these areas prior to sale:

1. An overall operational policy for the subsidiary during the sale period must be evolved.
2. When and how to inform employees and secure their assistance.
3. What personnel will be assigned to implement the sales program?
4. A review of the relationship with and obligations to prior shareholders is necessary if the subsidiary was recently acquired.
5. Will outside consultants be used in the program and, if so, who will they be?
6. Can available subsidiary financial data be relied upon and, if not, what steps will be taken to secure additional data?
7. What amounts of termination pay, if any, will be paid to employees?
8. What special bonuses, if any, will be paid key employees to assist in the sale and go with the new owner?
9. What obligations exist under pension schemes and how will these be treated?
10. What will be the seller's policy regarding employee benefits such as holidays, vacations, and group insurance, and what costs will the buyer be expected to assume?
11. What obligations exist under stock purchase, bonus, or option plans and how will these be treated?
12. What is the seller's position regarding who is responsible for commissions and incentive payments earned prior to closing but not payable until after closing?
13. What will be the internal procedures for establishing the bargaining latitude for the seller's negotiators, and what will be the approval procedures governing their activities?
14. What will be the official statement of why the subsidiary is for sale?
15. Who is responsible for communicating and answering questions about the sales program?
16. How will the public be informed and be kept informed of the program?

17. How will customers and the overall industry be informed of the sales program?
18. Are there obligations to former employees being paid from current funds?
19. Are there deferred compensation plans and how will these be treated?
20. Is the business dependent upon a small number of customers or suppliers and how will they be notified and retained?
21. Has the subsidiary been involved in any illegal activity?

Chapter 4
Defining What is For Sale

The seller must develop an accurate list of what is included in the sale, what is not, and what may or may not be included.

1. Does the seller understand fully the nature of each balance sheet item?
2. What assets and liabilities exist which are not reflected on the balance sheet and how will these be treated in the sale?
3. Will all subsidiary personnel be included and will any be specifically excluded?
4. Do any employees have a dual role of providing services to the subsidiary for sale and other parts of the corporation? How will this be handled after the sale?
5. What real estate is included?
6. Is all transportation equipment included?
7. Is any manufacturing equipment excluded?
8. Do any assets or investments unrelated to the basic business exist and will these be excluded?
9. Are all receivables to be included and at what value?
10. Are doubtful receivables included and at what value?
11. Are written-off receivables included?
12. Is all inventory included and at what value?
13. Will inventory written off as "worthless" be included?
14. Will surplus assets unnecessary to the present level of business be included?
15. Is the subsidiary's cash included?
16. Will mobilization payments, down payments, and progress payments be all or partially excluded?
17. What liabilities will be excluded?
    — losses on problem jobs?
    — debts to any creditors?

— intercompany debts?

— taxes due?

— payables?

18. Can some locations or parts of the business be excluded and retained, liquidated, or sold later?
19. Who will be responsible for product warranty?
20. Will patents be sold?
21. Will licensing agreements be transferred?
22. What trade names and trademarks are included?
23. Who will be responsible for current or potential litigation?
24. Who will receive insurance rebates or extra charges?
25. Will expensed items be included and how will they be valued?
26. How will accruals, reserves, and retentions be evaluated and treated?
27. What is the condition of the backlog and will it all be included?
28. Can less than 100% of the stock in the subsidiary be sold?
29. Can a division or product line for sale be restructured as a complete autonomous subsidiary?
30. What departments, personnel, or services are missing and needed to make the division or product line a complete going business?

Chapter 5
Pricing

1. Prior to setting a price, the seller must decide:
   — exactly what is for sale and what will be included in the sale
   — how the sale will be structured, sale of stock, assets only, selected assets and liabilities, etc.
2. How will price be affected by changes which occur in the financial condition of the company prior to closing.
3. What is the tax effect for various types of transaction structures and the consideration if received as cash, stock, notes or contingency payments?
4. What is the breakeven price for the seller?
   — from a financial accounting basis
   — from a cash after-tax basis
5. What is the true book value?
6. What could be received if the subsidiary was shut down and liquidated?
7. Develop a complete conceptual business plan for future operation of subsidiary supported by both profit and cash flow forecasts.

8. Calculate a price range using the following guidelines:

Low point of range = price that provides a return on investment in the second year of ownership
which is three times that received on
conservative investments such as high
grade corporate bonds.

High point of range = price that provides a return on investment in second year of ownership
which is 150% of that received on conservative investments such as high
grade corporate bonds.

9. Set a price within the range that is no greater than the sum of
the total earnings forecast for five years.
10. Does the price established meet the seller's objectives?
11. Is the price such that it will not dilute a buyer's earnings after
the first year?
12. What terms and currency will be acceptable?
— Types of consideration:
  (i) cash
  (ii) notes
  (iii) stock
  (iv) debentures
  (v) contingency payments
  (vi) merchandise credit
— What interest rates on notes will be acceptable?
— What will be the maximum duration of notes and frequency
of principal payments?
— Is the currency received convertible into hard currency and
can the proceeds from the sale be repatriated?
13. What is the buyer's downside risk with the established price?
14. Can the seller develop additional inducements to make the price
attractive such as continued or new business with the subsidiary or other business prospects between the seller and
buyer?
15. Should the price be reduced by retaining a minority interest?
16. Should large liabilities or potential unknown liabilities be
retained by the seller or to make a price acceptable?

Chapter 6
Organizing to Sell

1. Are the eight basic elements of a sales program thought out and
responsibility assigned?
— major decision making
— overall management

— day-to-day supervision
— data gathering
— contact of prospects and selling
— negotiating
— documentation and closing
— transition

2. What will be the role of the chief executive officer?
3. What is the role of group, divisional, or regional managers?
4. Who will be the executive assigned primary responsibility for planning and implementing the program?
5. Who will be the senior accountant assigned?
6. Who will provide legal assistance?
7. Who will be the principal negotiator?
8. What subsidiary personnel will be involved and in what role?
9. Will outside assistance be utilized?
   — consultants
   — investment bankers
   — business brokers
   — divestment specialists
10. Are controls established so that a brokerage or finder's fee obligation will not be incurred inadvertently?

Chapter 7
Developing the Sales Program

1. Why is the subsidiary for sale?
2. How will the rationale as to why the subsidiary is for sale be presented both externally and internally?
3. Has a complete valid economic rationale including a conceptual business plan been developed as to why someone should buy the subsidiary at the established price?
4. Have intangible and psychological factors as supplementary reasons for buying been developed?
5. What is the timing for the commencement of contacting prospects? Set a date.
6. Is an explanation available as to why the subsidiary is now for sale rather than at an earlier date?
7. How will prospects be treated who contact the seller before he is ready?
8. Are arrangements and control procedures established for access by prospects to the subsidiary's facilities?
9. How will negative aspects of the subsidiary be presented?
10. Are selling team personnel assignments clearly made?

11. Develop a short sales package containing:
    — product literature
    — description of subsidiary including its history
    — description of markets and industry served
    — addresses and list of subsidiary locations
    — individual to contact in the selling organization
    — description of unusual assets or other features of value
    — size indicated by sales volume and number of employees
12. Develop a longer package of sales literature containing:
    — everything found in the short package
    — financial statement
    — organization chart
    — description of company competitive position
    — description of any valuable patents or licenses
13. What financing can be arranged for a buyer?
14. Develop volumes containing data, decisions, and answers to all applicable questions in Appendix A, B, and C.

Chapter 8
Employees are Assets

1. Develop an overall program designed to retain subsidiary employees for the new owner.
2. Develop a program of two-way communication with the subsidiary employees during the sales program.
3. What is the attitude of the subsidiary employees toward the contemplated sale and the parent company in general?
4. Develop policies regarding all employee compensation and benefit programs and explain these policies to the subsidiary employees.
5. Will any termination payments or special bonuses be paid?
6. How much can subsidiary employees be allowed to talk with prospects?
7. How will unsolicited assistance from subsidiary personnel be treated?

Chapter 9
Prospects

1. Enlist the aid of all possible to identify prospects; seller's executives, regional or divisional managers, members of the selling team, subsidiary employees, attorneys, accountants and friends of the company, industrial commissions, foreign governments, banks, and creditors.

2. Reason out what type businesses would be most logical prospects.
3. Secure all public and private data available for each prospect.
4. Screen prospects once identified to eliminate those without the necessary financial qualifications.
5. The following are possible prospects:
   — non-U.S. banks
   — creditors
   — foreign governments
   — foreign government officials
   — manufacturers' representatives
   — foreign marketing companies
   — related equipment manufacturers or service organizations
   — companies selling to the same customers
   — suppliers
   — licensors and licensees
   — customers and clients
   — former shareholders
   — joint venture partners
   — employees
   — competitors
   — similar businesses in other areas
   — companies specializing in parts and services
   — companies specializing in buying divestitures
   — promotional type companies
   — minority shareholders
   — prospects interested in buying less than 100%
   — the man next door
6. Prepare files on each prospect.
7. Check out prospects for their character, integrity and financial ability.

Chapter 10
Final Preparations

The subsidiary should be given its best possible appearance through improvements and resolution of problems.

1. Make certain ownership of the subsidiary and all assets are consistent with the tax program and sale structure.
2. Clean-up the subsidiary's physical facilities.
3. Maintain an effective housekeeping program.
4. Dispose of scrap and waste.

5. Dispose of any surplus assets not currently being used in the business.
6. Collect slow receivables.
7. Review written-off receivables to determine if any have become collectible.
8. Tighten control on credit procedures.
9. Review all contracts, licensing agreements, sales agreements, leases, and franchises to determine if they have expired or are about to expire.
10. Reduce inventory to the lowest practical level.
11. Dispose of written-off inventory.
12. Set up a records retention program. Decide what records are to go with the sale and what must be duplicated.
13. Resolve pending litigation and determine its exact status and probable outcome.
14. Resolve all warranty or service claims possible; and if not possible, determine extent of exposure.
15. Maintain if possible, a stable management group in the subsidiary.
16. Avoid new long-term commitments with suppliers.
17. Clean up Wage & Hour, OSHA, EPA, and EEO violations or any other government problems.

Chapter 11
Contact and Follow-Up

1. Contact most probable prospects first.
2. Do not have more prospects active at a time than can be processed.
3. Critique each prospect contact to learn of ways to improve sales presentation.
4. Determine the best person to contact in each prospect's organization.
5. After determining the best executive in the prospect's organization to contact, review again all information on the prospect. Be sensitive to avoid situations where contacting one person offends others.
6. Basic methods of first contact:
   — face-to-face meeting
   — telephone contact
   — mail with sales contact follow-up
7. Are third party contacts possible?
8. Maintain complete written reports of all contacts.

9. Supply promptly information requested by prospects. Are procedures set up for doing so?
10. How will business brokers volunteering their services be treated?
11. What is the sophistication of the prospect's representatives?
12. Are personnel involved for both the buyer and the seller of equal rank?
13. What is the internal power structure of the prospect and what is their informal and formal decision making procedure?
14. Once a prospect rejects the proposal, can he be revived?
15. The letter of intent should be the first objective. Has one been drafted?
16. How will competing prospects be handled?
17. How will employees and the public be notified of an agreement?

Index

NOTES